ON TEMPELHOFER FELD

SPECTOR BOOKS

On Tempelhofer Feld

BENJAMIN DEBOOSERE
WOUTER DE RAEVE
(Eds.)

SPECTOR BOOKS

TABLE OF CONTENTS

When we first set foot on Tempelhofer Feld in 2012, we were immediately overwhelmed by the dynamics of this extraordinary and unique place. Its informal use and minimal infrastructural amenities generated a precarious balance between the planned and unplanned, between routine and freedom. The prevailing, mainly economic approach to space seemed not to apply. This visit to the former airport signaled the start of our search for alternative ways of shaping our space.

In autumn 2008, the last plane departed from Berlin's Tempelhof Airport. From then on, a sturdy fence closed the site off from its surroundings and guaranteed that this immense open space in the middle of the city remained untouched. Several neighborhood groups and activists voiced their concerns about this "lost space." Together they set up a protest campaign under the slogan "Have you ever squatted an airport?" Their aim was to collectively climb the fence and occupy the field. A huge number of police officers were summoned from all over Germany to prevent the squatters from doing so. Soon after, in 2010, the Senate of Berlin decided to open up Tempelhofer Feld for public use, though subject to certain conditions. In the meantime, the public and the media continued to speculate on the possible use of the site. Several proposals had been put forward, the most interesting and thoroughly considered of which arose out of the cooperation between the experimental architectural practices of raumlabor and Urban Catalyst studio. They generated a "procedural development concept" for transformation that allowed the site to evolve—over a period spanning several years or even decades—in a close relationship with its immediate surroundings and with the developments taking place on a larger scale throughout Berlin.

Michael Müller, at that time Berlin's senator for urban development and the environment, had other plans for what he had baptized Tempelhofer Freiheit.[1] His scenario was based on a more traditional notion of urban development, with a focus on short-term profit, competition between cities, and an economic system based on tourism, recreation, and consumption. Claiming this would address the city's housing issue, the Berlin Senate planned to subdivide the site and build on part of it. The remaining open space would be arranged as a "designer park" of which "all other European cities would be jealous."[2]

One phase of Urban Catalyst studio and raumlabor's procedural development concept, the so-called pioneer stage, was to focus on the temporary use of the

1 The Berlin Senate for Urban Development and the Environment had renamed Tempelhofer Feld as Tempelhofer Freiheit. The same name was given to the organization managing their development plan.

2 "Tempelhofer Freiheit is a blessing for Berlin, and one that will make other cities simply go green with envy." Michael Müller, then senator for Urban Development and the Environment, cited in a Tempelhofer Freiheit leaflet "Park Landscape Development," collected at Tempelhofer Feld, July 19, 2012.

site as inspiration for its further development. It was implemented in the governmental plans, or rather, recuperated under the guise of participation. The local cooperation with neighborhood residents, artistic interventions, and ecological and innovative activities gave the appearance of civil involvement, while the actual future of the site had already been decided.

The citizens' initiative 100% Tempelhofer Feld arose as a response to the Senate's development plans. The initiative saw Tempelhofer Feld as *ein Feld für alle*: a field for all, an open space 100 percent free of building development and privatization. For several years 100% Tempelhofer Feld raised awareness with protest actions, information evenings, and media campaigning. But when it came to the Berlin authorities, their message fell on deaf ears. As a result, 100% Tempelhofer Feld decided to ensure its voice be heard by organizing a referendum, and in May 2014 the citizen's initiative won its case. At first sight this seemed to be a good thing. If the Senate of Berlin were to implement its project, the emphasis would, as Kenny Cupers puts it, be on public order, efficiency, and profitability, leading to a controlled, mono-functional, and aseptic space.[3]

The referendum could have opened the door to the formation of a forceful spatial vision, but it did not succeed in this. The question put to the referendum was phrased so that the site would have to be

3 Cf. Kenny Cupers, "Promises of a Free Space," in *Openbaarheid*, Cahier #3, edited by Vlaams Bouwmeester (Brussels, 2011), 208.

maintained in its present state. The debate shifted from the potential of spatial research by design to the management of an open green space.[4] Reflection on the future of Tempelhofer Feld was limited to a polarized debate in which citizens were forced to choose between the Berlin Senate's view and that of the citizens' initiative: the choice between building or not building, or between a clear city-marketing program and leaving the place untouched.

In 2013, one year after our first encounter with this extraordinary space, we had the opportunity to study the case of Tempelhofer Feld in the context of a four-month artistic residency at Air Berlin Alexanderplatz. It was never our intention to develop yet another alternative design for Tempelhofer Feld but rather to employ this case study as a starting point for reflecting on the interaction between societal urgencies and spatial practice. On Tempelhofer Feld one could witness first-hand the current state of democracy, the different actors involved, and the manner in which they interact and aim to overcome one another.

This publication consists of two volumes. The first volume compiles a photographic record of Tempelhofer Feld. At first sight the pictures celebrate the temporariness of the field, emphasized by the use of

4 Katharine Burgess, "Community Participation in Parks Development: Two Examples from Berlin," *The Nature of Cities* (December 10, 2014), accessed June 10, 2015, http://www.thenatureofcities.com/2014/12/10/community-participation-in-parks-development-two-examples-from-berlin/.

black and white. But the second volume, a pocket book that functions as a reader assembling a selection of conversations contextualizing and critically addressing the space, offers a more nuanced interpretation. Taking an artistic rather than an academic approach and with a necessary pinch of naivety and boldness, we intruded into the existing field of spatial expertise and social theory, and engaged in conversations with architects, philosophers, geographers, and sociologists from Berlin and Brussels, our home city. With every conversation, we saw the everyday reality of Tempelhofer Feld, captured in the photographs, in a new light.

Looking back today, the residency functioned as a self-organized educational program. It served as a breeding ground for reflections on the kind of strategies that might be required to enable social, progressive, and humane visions of society to penetrate to the heart of power. We hope that these texts and images may also inspire the reader and contribute to a broader and more fundamental contemplation of how we, individually and collectively, can be genuinely involved in the way our society develops.

Benjamin Deboosere and Wouter De Raeve,
March 2016

Erkundung — Explorative Urbanism

MARKUS BADER

July 2013, Berlin

DEBOOSERE / DE RAEVE:

Together with Klaus Overmeyer of Urban Catalyst studio, you developed a procedural development concept for Tempelhofer Feld. How did this cooperation come about?

At the end of 2006, the urbanism firm MBUP, which was involved in preparatory studies for Tempelhofer Feld, organized a short workshop with associates from three practices: landscape architects from Halle an der Saale, Urban Catalyst studio, and us (raumlabor). It was presented as a workshop, but it was basically an informal competition. We competed with each other over ideas we had developed. It was then that we realized that we were on the same page as Urban Catalyst studio. Although we delivered our expertise, we didn't receive any reply from either MBUP or the Senate Department for Urban Development and the Environment. About six months later, in 2007, Klaus Overmeyer and I discussed how strange this silence was. Naturally, the workshop generated more questions than answers, and we were curious about what was going to happen with our ideas. Since we felt it would be wiser to put the remaining time to good use, I suggested to Klaus that we forget about the competition and join forces. We put our ideas together and quickly got excited about the discussions that took shape and the concepts we developed. We made time and process diagrams that illustrated our current position, the point at which the airport would cease to operate, and how we could start talking about the conversion of the space from one form to another.

How did you manage to work your way into collaboration with the Senate of Berlin?

At the time, the board of directors of the Senate Department for Urban Development and the Environment was going through a reshuffle, with Mr. Stimmann, who had quite a conservative and top-down approach, being replaced by Mrs. Lüscher, who is still in charge. In contrast to her predecessor, she is more interested in a procedural approach in the context of urban transformation. This triggered an enthusiasm within the planning office, and this shift meant that things could be addressed accordingly. After Klaus and I had joined forces, we initiated a dialogue between our own practices, MBUP, and representatives from the Senate Department for Urban Development and the Environment. As a result of these conversations, the

Ideenwerkstatt Tempelhof (Tempelhof ideas workshop) team was formed and asked to develop a framework for the initial stages of the development process.

What was the result of your work?

The result was a beautiful, thick office folder containing a concept for a system of operation for the site. It is one of those files you store on a shelf. It is full of expertise, good ideas, and sketches. We tried to review all the issues that we considered important: we did not merely focus on urban development as such, but on financial and organizational aspects, and we also tried to develop a full understanding of what a city must do to set a project like this in motion. That was a process that took two years (2007–9), with a lot of dialogue with the representatives from the Senate Department for Urban Development and the Environment. Throughout this process we also organized conferences and workshops with experts from outside the city and the representatives of municipal planning. One seminar focused on the basic question, What is the situation at hand, and how do we deal with it? A second workshop considered the fact that the end of Tempelhofer Feld as an airport was approaching and examined how to take the first step into this unknown territory.

What were some of the ideas you developed?

Primarily, we recommended a smooth and immediate transition between the end of Tempelhof as an airport and the onset of its new function. We suggested a phase we called *Erkundung* (exploration), a culturally-oriented phase following the closure of the airport, in which basic infrastructural matters such as safety issues could be developed. While preparations for the actual opening were finalized, we suggested that a limited audience be allowed on site in order to experience the field. The idea of *Erkundung* was to present a different view of the field in response to the public's perception of loss— the fact of losing this inner-city airport—which was strong throughout Berlin at the time.[1] People seemed to be terrified by the idea that there was no explanation and no concept about what would happen to this former airport. In *Erkundung*, we aimed to immediately oppose the experience of loss by replacing it with a new kind of encounter, an artistic approach, evoking the imagination of what the site could become.

This phase was not realized, one reason being the lack of funding. I assume that there was political fear involved behind the scenes. After the referendum against the closure of the airport, a decision was made to keep everything calm for a while. It was only in May 2010, two years after its closure, that the field was opened to the public. During the interim phase, nothing really happened. The Senate of Berlin took its time in developing the organizational model currently in place.

Was it the idea of the Berlin Senate to open the site to the public before defining its future purpose?

There are always divergent opinions concerning a project of this size. Some supported a full and immediate opening, while others were completely against it. They wanted to have a detailed plan first and only then consider allowing the public in. They feared that as soon as it was made public it would be hard to retrieve it again for another use. For example, if the city decided to proceed with housing developments on the site. More politicians were convinced that the airport should be opened, possibly because of the public pressure behind the Have You Ever Squatted an Airport? demonstration in mid-2009. The closure had by then cost an estimated one million euro in defensive measures. Otherwise they would have had to invest more and more to protect it against intruders and activists.

1 Tempelhofer Feld is not only important in the history of aviation, but is also internationally known for its important role in Cold War history as the base for airlifts during the Berlin Blockade (1948–49). Therefore, when it was announced that the airport would be shut down, many people considered this a loss to the city, and a referendum against its closure was organized. However, it didn't engage enough voters to succeed.

Did your master plan include a final interpretation of what Tempelhofer Feld should become?

No, we didn't fix a final goal or image. What we proposed was a dynamic master plan. We suggested that people in Berlin be allowed on the field, not simply as visitors, but to really engage them as co-developers and co-inventors of the space. We wanted to facilitate an organic process to determine what should happen and connect the grassroots way of developing a site to a more traditional planning method. We suggested that we could function as intermediaries between the planners and the users by following developments on site and communicating with the planning office. In this way, instead of going out and talking to people—something they do not usually do anyhow—the planners could follow the developments taking place on the field by looking at a sheet of paper. At the same time, the users—people engaging directly with the site were called "the pioneers"—would know that their actions would be represented in the development's plans.

Could you further describe this pioneer concept?

Our concept of urban pioneers made one fundamental offer to people: to engage with the site for a longer period. There is a lot of brief and ephemeral use of Tempelhofer Feld: people have barbecues, walk their dogs, fly kites or model airplanes, and so on. Such activities take place in the course of a few hours or more, up to a whole day. In the "pioneer process," people can stay on site for a longer period of time to pursue their own activities. This practice of experimental and explorative—meaning open-ended—use of space was common in Berlin, when the economic situation allowed spaces to be available for appropriation. Many spaces were used by squatters, and alternative arrangements were made with landlords, with at most low rents being paid. In the case of Tempelhofer Feld, we had the feeling that it would be exciting to discuss and explore what happened if a public development embraced this sort of personal initiative and tried to create a hybrid of different planning cultures. Not individuals or groups of people creating a little paradise for themselves but a new way of making a shared, public field. I do not think that this had ever been part of any official city development policy before. The pioneer process can be understood as a merge of informal practices and participation as part of top-down developments. This offers a new form of governance in the public sphere. A new distribution of responsibilities, propositions, and decision-making can take shape.

Just before discussions about Tempelhofer Feld emerged, the Gleisdreieck Park was developed. This was a gigantic project with an immense investment. There was an extensive participation process involving neighbors and other interest groups. However, the park resulted in a thoroughly designed public green area, with an emphasis on "designed." Participation on a large scale resulted in people's ideas being more or less included in the final design of the park. A number of programmatic inlays, which are run by neighborhood associations and groups, were only included on a much smaller scale.

Tempelhofer Feld does not look designed, and I would argue that this is one of its prime qualities. It feels more like it was found. What is nice about this "found" quality, for me as a city dweller, is that it seems more accessible. It is not about the so-called good guys in politics and planning departments that supplied something for us, the users. It is about the opportunity to feel more like someone who appropriates and co-creates, rather than someone who just enacts behaviors that have already been inscribed into a space.

The Senate Department for Urban Development and the Environment adopted the idea of the pioneer project. Did it turn out the way you imagined?

I have an ambiguous feeling about it. In our proposal, the pioneer process was more directly linked to an agency that coordinates the urban pioneer process and acts as translator and agent, giving the process its own organizational structure. This would potentially have provided the pioneers with more negotiation power to counter the top-down approach of Tempelhofer Freiheit, the organization commissioned by the Senate for the development.[2] Now, the pioneer process is integrated into Tempelhofer Freiheit.

2 After the referendum in 2014, the name "Tempelhofer Freiheit" was removed from the field and the process. It now stands for the phase when development was intended to take the form of housing and a "designer park."

Another decision I cannot fully agree with is that all the activities hosted on the field have to be noncommercial. This is quite counterproductive if you want to develop something out of nothing to support people. It makes it a space in which only leisure activities or events that have external sponsorship can take place. It would be far more interesting to say: "Why not grow plants, for example, and sell them? Why not create small economic opportunities? Or let's sell some drinks to the people enjoying our built environment so as to refinance some of the material we brought in—or to cover the 5,000 euro annual rent." Sadly, these are exactly the sorts of things Tempelhofer Freiheit has restricted.

I'm also not a fan of the way they have allocated the projects. The development company promoted the idea of a "themed urbanism." They divided the field into separate zones: a socially themed sector close to Neukölln, a religiously themed area close to the Turkish Cemetery and the Şehitlik Mosque, a culturally themed site in the area toward the north, an educationally themed space to the west, and an area related to ecological technologies in the south. To group them accordingly, the development company asked the initiatives which themes their proposals would fit into. Consequently, instead of cultural actors, environmental activists and people with knowledge of technical stuff sitting together around a campfire and developing and exchanging ideas, their involvement is divided into segmented sites on the field. This makes it really tough for groups to create and develop a sort of community organization, which is one of the main reasons we wanted to invite and bring people together in the first place.

So our plan was integrated in a highly modified way, while still portraying this image of a nice, self-made, co-working, co-existing, communing collaboration of all these happy "co-" words. But I do not believe this was done with bad intentions. I'm in favor of dialogue and communication. For example, the very leftist and straightforward political activists that manage the urban gardening project are working with people from Tempelhofer Freiheit. Conversation is important in cities. If we head only for controversy and conflict, nothing will improve.

What do you think about the master plan for Tempelhofer Feld presented by the Berlin Senate?

It basically depicts the field with built structures around the edges, and a big green core, namely a park. This inner part is the least convincing to me. The winning scheme for the landscape competition organized by the Berlin Senate presents a pretty thorough redesign, with new pathways, trees, and geometries.[3] What I am mostly interested in is the idea of people entering a field that functions as a sort of free space. I do not think new paths or a new topography could increase the quality of the site. Seemingly trespassing a former airport and being able to walk on a 40 m wide runway is already fantastic. The landscape architecture competition was obviously aimed at something quite different: to shape public investment into a park. Once installed, the park could be left alone and maintained by the park manager. The public's role is being reduced to that of the end user, not the co-inventor. It is therefore even less the design and rather the underlying governance models that are in conflict.

I believe you have to radically mix up the role descriptions. If you reframe human activities—who it is that takes care of the site, how it is being shaped, and so on—many other futures become imaginable.

A recurring discussion is constantly developing around the conflict between public investment and private initiative. The 100% Tempelhofer Feld action group proposed an idea with which to open up the debate: of the 65 million euro that is the current investment in the park, each Berliner should get 20 euro and one square meter. Individuals could combine their square meters with someone else's and create something together. Of course it is just an idea, but the concept of ownership is important in this context. Not in terms of property ownership for people to put up a fence, so to speak, but ownership centered on the notion of involvement. That is a different kind of own-

3 This design was conducted by a British team that included landscape architecture company GROSS. MAX. and Sutherland Hussey Architects. Their plan puts the main focus on aesthetics instead of content, with a very narrow view of participation. This becomes painfully clear in a lecture by Eelco Hooftman of GROSS. MAX. at the Walker Art Center, Minneapolis, about the origin of his plans for Tempelhofer Feld. This lecture was held on May 9, 2013, and can be seen on http://youtu.be/jJN_ehnuUn8, accessed July 14, 2015.

ership and that is what I am interested in. Following this line of reasoning, you can discuss ownership not only regarding spaces and objects, but also regarding the dynamics of a place: the maintenance and a general sense of belonging, to mention just two very soft aims.

What is your opinion of the building plans?

I don't want to proclaim that there should be no building development whatsoever and that Tempelhofer Feld must stay free and open. My suggestion is that it is probably more interesting to engage people in a debate on what to build and to take this process as an opportunity to have an open discussion about public development. By losing part of its openness, I think a lot of good ideas were formulated from which the field would benefit. The neighborhoods around Tempelhofer Feld are very diverse and an architectural intervention might help them come together—but not at all in the way the Berlin Senate's plans lay it out.

Would it be possible to change the Berlin Senate's current vision for Tempelhofer Feld and would you be able to get involved once again?

No, I don't think so. As they say in German, *die Messen sind gesungen* (it's too late). The wheels are turning and will lead to the creation of a park. The Berlin Senate is very well aware of the fact that many citizens do not welcome this change because they are happy with the current situation. Therefore they decided to not create the park immediately, but to change things gradually. They want to turn the building site into something likeable. There was even a call for ideas put out to architects to submit proposals for this process.

I believe the only counterforce could come from the way the space is used. If exciting uses materialize, things might turn out quite differently.

Additional note by Markus Bader in 2015 Since the referendum in 2014, things have changed fundamentally. Berlin now has a THF-Gesetz (THF law) that forbids any development. My analysis in our interview was quite accurate: many of the 100% Tempelhofer Feld activists and supporters were or are involved in the pioneer process. The opportunity for productive negotiation was not taken on by the development agency between 2010 and 2014; instead they pursued a policy of "please keep hanging on while we take decisions." As a result, the conflict escalated, which led to the referendum.

It would take a more exhaustive analysis to establish why this was able to happen. I believe the 78% rise in rents in Neukölln—a district neighboring Tempelhofer Feld—between 2008 and 2014 can be seen as an indicator of what has been happening in the city since the financial crisis: speculation that has increased house prices and rents, further fueled by a growing number of inhabitants. This changes the climate in Berlin. There is a growing fear of being evicted from your home or place of business for economic reasons.

Evaluating these events, we must ask ourselves, What is essential for a collaborative and inclusive urban development? Trust? True arenas of negotiation are needed, such as where disputes can publicly take place and the dialogue on urban futures is kept transparent and open. I believe it is precisely such emotional elements as trust that are at the heart of developing new models of urban governance. Since the referendum, the powers have been redistributed, but the same challenges and questions of development and participation remain urgent.

Temporary Use Berlin

PHILIPP OSWALT

November 2013, Berlin

DEBOOSERE / DE RAEVE:

How does temporary use correlate with the history of Berlin?

After 1945, Berlin was no longer the capital of Germany and was divided into East and West Berlin. This historic turning point as well as severe destruction by aerial bombardment led to a decline in the population of about a million. An important spatial consequence was the appearance of huge voids in the inner city. Various modes of temporary use emerged in these spaces, which were devoted, amongst other things, to food cultivation, the construction of makeshift housing, and leisure activities.

In the 1960s, instead of refurbishing existing housing stock, the governments—first in the West and then in the East—addressed the housing issue with the construction of new mass housing on the outskirts of the city. This led to an enormous number of rundown houses in the inner city and sparked a new boom in temporary use that saw squats mushroom across vast swaths of abandoned city blocks.

In 1989, when the Wall fell, the government left office causing a fissure in East Berlin between existing regulations and new property-control policies. As it took time to establish new structures, this was the opportunity for many people—mainly those who had just moved to Berlin—to make use of the vacant spaces. The squatting movement began in the district of Mitte and subsequently spread to Prenzlauer Berg and Friedrichshain.

New governmental and real-estate structures quickly put limits on this "extreme freedom," which lasted only for a year or two. However, with real-estate development being a slow and capital-absorbing process, temporary use continued for the next twenty years.

How did temporary use manifest itself during this later period?

The vacant spaces formed zones of experimental use in the city, with a wide spectrum of activities taking place—gardens, trailer camps, markets, sports, and different forms of recreation. Cultural and nightlife attractions developed and with them came new lifestyles, like punk culture. This resulted in the now-legendary club and art scene.

What was the reaction to this from the planners' perspective?

Oswald Mathias Ungers's 1977 project *The City within the City: Berlin as Green Archipelago*[1] examined what a shrinking city might look like. He experienced the decline of New York, in the wake of its suburbanization and bankruptcy. Although a very different story, it influenced him in his work. *The City within the City* was proposed for the 1987 IBA (International Architecture Exhibition). However, Josef Paul Kleihues prevailed with his idea of "re-establishing the city fabric." His concept was a well-ordered and well-regulated urban planning policy based on the idea of reconstructing the city layout of the nineteenth century.[2]

In the 1990s, the conservative view on urbanism radicalized when Hans Stimmann became Senate Building Director. It was no longer solely about reconstructing the fabric of the city—now architecture itself also became regulated. The rule was to follow a kind of "Berlin style of architecture" based on a pseudo-historical design. From 2000 on, this completely fake style turned even more radical, with the literal reconstruction of buildings that at one time or another had, for various reasons, fallen into disrepair. From this point on, the intention was to erase the history of the twentieth century completely—reinventing the past by ignoring the most difficult episode of German history. But, to a large extent, this concept remained a pipe dream, as a city on the scale of Berlin cannot be remodeled and controlled so easily.

Despite official policies, temporary use was actually the main component in shaping the city and dominating its cultural and urban development. Outside of the professional discourse, urban life came

1 The manifesto from 1977 was recently republished as *The City in the City–Berlin: A Green Archipelago* (Lars Müller Publishers, 2013). "With *The City within the City* Oswald Mathias Ungers and a number of his colleagues from Cornell University presented the first concepts and intellectual models for the shrinking city." Lars Müller Publishers, accessed July 9, 2015, www.lars-mueller-publishers.com/en/die-stadt-in-der-stadt.

2 The attitude of "removing traces of history in the name of history" was criticized by Rem Koolhaas, among others, as being nostalgic.

much more into play than the new architectural ideologies. Nonetheless, it took urban planners more than a decade to develop an understanding of this fact.

When we started our project researching Tempelhofer Feld, we had the feeling that the administration was supportive toward process-based planning initiatives, relative to your work and that of other architectural practices. But this doesn't seem to have been the case.

As I just mentioned, temporary use in the 1990s occurred independently from and parallel to official planning, official discourse, and even the architectural profession. Nothing was accepted or initiated by the public administration in a broader sense, so it's no great surprise that the administration wasn't on the same page. They almost completely ignored it—one exception was the presentation of the Berlin club scene at the World Fair Expo 2000 in Hanover. However, it did not make any link to urban planning. The first real instance of a project offering insights into temporary use and confronting the public with its possibilities was our Volkspalast 2004. This generated a new discourse, which slowly influenced and changed the attitudes of official policies. Finally, in 2007, the Senate commissioned one of the first books and exhibitions on temporary use authored by my colleague Klaus Overmeyer: *Urban Pioneers* (Jovis Verlag, 2007). This was based on research conducted by our Urban Catalyst collective.

Would it be possible to generate greater awareness of the notion of process-based planning in the administrative departments?

First of all, I believe we should not disregard everything we know about classical planning. It is an achievement, it did not exist forever, and it generated a certain body of valuable knowledge. However, the idea of control over the final result and a top-down approach unquestionably needs to be redefined, which means gaining a new understanding of the role of the state, the public, users, investors, and every actor involved in a spatial development plan. While some within the professional architectural realm have been reflecting on this issue, the political discourse is not yet on the same page. City administrations traditionally tend to be conservative with an unhealthy propensity to crave control, and they can find it hard to open up to experimentation. But then again, they are not all homogenous. Within this rigid structure, there is a minority of people who are maneuvering around bureaucratic routine, pushing traditional policies, and not following the official agenda . For example, in the early 1990s, Jutta Waitz of the Wohnungsbaugesellschaft Mitte (Housing Association Mitte) mobilized her position to enable a lot of uses and activities outside of the official agenda. Another example was that, during the Volks-palast 2004 project,[3] we collaborated with Dorothee Durbrau, the District Counselor for City Development in Berlin-Mitte and Thomas Flierl, Senator for Science, Research, and Culture. One can often find an alliance within parts of the administration.

Considering its status and symbolic value, the Palast der Republik seemed to be an impossible space in which to initiate temporary use. Was it your aim to formulate an alternative to the development plans at that point?

It was a very difficult and long struggle, but we finally succeeded. And yes, everybody involved was trying to have an impact on the future development of the site, giving the chance for alternatives to

3 Volkspalast 2004 initiated temporary cultural use in the Palast der Republik, "the former capital building of the German Democratic Republic. It was built after WWII on the site where the heavily damaged castle of the city, the 'Stadt Schloss,' once stood. After the fall of the GDR regime a debate ensued [about] whether the 'Palast der Republik' should be rehabilitated or whether it should be torn down and replaced by something else—building a copy of the old castle was the preferred solution." Volkspalast 2004 was a "proposal for changing the paradigm of the debate around the Palast," shifting "the focus from the facade to the usage." See Amelie Deuflhard and Sophie Krempl-Klieeisen, "Volkspalast: History of an Interim Usage. Art–Intervention–Activism–Transformation," trans. Benjamin Weinthal, mu·dot, accessed August 10, 2015, http://www.monu.org/monu4/Volkspalast.pdf.

emerge, different from the erasure of the Palast and the reconstruction of the castle. With Fun Palace Berlin 200X[4] we also explicitly addressed these questions. We did not formulate a final plan, of course, but instead initiated an open-ended process. Even so, we did not succeed in having an impact on the current redesign of the Palast der Republik. Nevertheless, when looking back, I think the general influence of this project was substantial, and that it benefited a lot from the enormous prominence of the site.

Was your involvement in the Palast der Republik debate self-initiated? Or how did it occur?

After my return to Berlin from the Netherlands, where I had been working for the architecture firms OMA and MVRDV, I was no longer interested in critiquing absurd architectural policies. Instead, I wanted to formulate a positive vision. I loved Berlin and wanted to develop another conceptual understanding of this city. Together with Anthony Fontenot, an American friend of mine who also worked at OMA, we developed the idea for the book *Berlin – Stadt ohne Form* (Prestel Verlag, 2000). Temporality was one of the nine subjects of the book. Landscape architect Klaus Overmeyer—another friend of mine—and I discussed the possibility of developing the subject further and successfully obtained European funding to continue our thinking. The project was expected to be an all-in-one solution, or, as we say in German, an *eierlegende Wollmilchsau* ("the pig that lays eggs and produces wool and milk"). It had to be research-based and have a practical application further down the line. It also had to involve the different municipalities and be economically viable.

4 "In October 2004 [Urban Catalyst] brought together guests from around the world to participate in an open brainstorming, conducted in the Palace of the Republic in Berlin. The conference was curated by an international team consisting of Philipp Misselwitz, Hans-Ulrich Obrist, Philipp Oswalt and Stefan Rethfeld. The conference and related events were inspired by the groundbreaking work of the architect and thinker Cedric Price (1934–2003) and in particular his radical unrealized architectural vision for a Fun Palace (1961–1966). Participants were invited to develop ideas and proposals in [the] form of public statements." Urban Catalyst, accessed July 6, 2015, www.urbancatalyst.net/xideen.php?lang=en.

For a Berlin case study, we chose the area around Ostbahnhof in Friedrichshain, where there was a huge variety and varying intensities of temporary use. But when we started to develop models for integrating temporary use into urban development and planning, the mayor of Friedrichshain-Kreuzberg, a member of Die Grünen (the Green Party), was not interested at all and refused any involvement, practical action, or collaboration.

At that point in time, the debate about the Palast der Republik was intensifying, and since we had to relocate our area of investigation, we decided to shift our focus to this case. We formed a team with six cultural partners and obtained political support from Thomas Flierl and Dorothee Dubrau, both of whom I mentioned earlier—but even so, the national administration kept blocking everything and left no room for negotiation. The Palast is a national symbol, and introducing cultural activities opens the door for things that might get out of control. It was a highly charged political conflict, and in order to gain the interest of the policy-makers, we were forced to initiate a public discourse. So we did exactly that and started a media campaign, set up exhibitions, and organized press conferences, etc. Meanwhile the pressure on the administration kept increasing. The public discourse, together with the enormous support from the media, changed the debate and finally opened the door for the Palast der Republik project.

Keeping in mind Volkspalast 2004, would it be interesting to reopen the debate concerning the future of Tempelhofer Feld?

The Palast der Republik was a rewarding test case—it was politically charged, very symbolic, and widely reported on by the press and media. Now it is gone without a physical trace, but I think that the project has contributed to a change in the discourse on temporary use. Tempelhofer Feld is well known, widely discussed, and carefully observed as well, and although it is not such an extreme case as the Palast, I do believe it could serve as a model or source of inspiration. Opening up the debate could have an impact on the broader understanding of urban planning.

What is your opinion of the current plans for Tempelhofer Feld?

It makes no sense to continue focusing on the struggle to keep the field free from any development; we should rather discuss what kind of development we would be interested in. The conventional design of the current plan is rooted in a classic landscape-design philosophy. There are examples of different, much more interesting and much more advanced approaches, not only in the Berlin tradition, like raumlabor and Urban Catalyst, but also many others. During the last ten years, the discourse on planning methodology has steered towards a better understanding of the possibilities offered by process-based planning. The designer is aware of and acknowledges the importance of the actors involved in the development. His actions are no longer mainly guided by aesthetic questions. Instead of defining a final result, the actors should be given a more active role. Still, we have to remain critical of the term "participation"—rather than sitting in a discussion to see what should be done, I would be more interested in having the actual possibility of doing something. In our consumer-oriented society, we look at people as merely consumers, whereas we should also look at them as producers. Berlin has a fine tradition and culture in this respect, and it would, to a large extent, be challenging to develop a project on Tempelhofer Feld based on this kind of philosophy. One of the problems is that urban development involves enormous amounts of capital, so it is mostly only people with huge financial resources that have an impact on what is happening.

Networked Spatiality

ERIC CORIJN

August 2013, Brussels

DEBOOSERE / DE RAEVE:

In what urban context can we situate a place such as Tempelhofer Feld?

After the Second World War, cities developed largely on the basis of a modernist concept whose two most significant characteristics were functionality and zoning. Living, working, recreation, and transport were all allotted separate spaces. This functional separation was accompanied by suburbanization, where the ideal life was played out in peripheral residential areas. The city center was considered above all as a commercial area and a service and user zone where people from outside the city could come to work, to shop, or for entertainment. Berlin is a perfect example of a city where a huge amount of space has been set aside for transport, space that was not intended for pleasant strolls. So a sort of anti-urbanity now prevails.

The present postindustrial economy is also played out in the city, but it is on a smaller scale, is more flexible, and functions via networks rather than institutions. It is in the first place a service sector and in most cases involves smaller companies that are linked together rather than one gigantic company such as Fiat, which at one time employed forty thousand workers on a single site. As a result of this, more places in the city have to be connected together, and this cuts across the old spatial planning of single-function sectors. The postindustrial city mixes production sites with living and consumer areas. This makes the urban fabric more complex. Division by function is replaced by the development of several nodal points. This gives rise to a polycentric urbanity that can best be captured in "mental maps." Unlike the modern industrial city, the new city is composed, in part, of a spatiality that has grown organically.

In addition, the social geography of the city has also become more complex. The old workers' neighborhoods have vanished, and the labor movement has gone with them. Instead, we now see less defined and fewer socially organized groups of people who are looking for their place in the city. A transition is thus occurring in which the old industrial functions, which occupied certain spaces in the city, are disappearing. This results in transitional zones that are impossible to fill in using a modernist approach. Take Tempelhofer Feld, for example. It would be impractical to drop a new monofunctional residential area into this space, which is right in the middle of the city.

How does this evolution impact the work of architects and the designers of master plans?

Master planning based on a blueprint aimed toward an end result has become obsolete. Programs are sought that are composed of process and coproduction planning methods. The most enlightened administrators and planners do not immediately allocate a use to major spaces in the urban network. They allow for temporary use and experiment.

Urban action groups have also changed. Small-scale actions link up with one another and this becomes a different form of organization than that of the main social protagonists. This flexibility must also take spatial form somewhere. Many sites in Berlin have become experimental developments like this, with a lot of self-steering.

At first sight, Tempelhofer Feld seems to be part of an enlightened planning vision, but when the proposal formulated by the government is studied just a bit more closely, it becomes clear that it is merely sugarcoated.

Administrators are guardians of a system who have to "manage" and who prefer stability, social harmony, and a spatial overview with clear functionality. The moment Tempelhofer Feld becomes a park, for instance, a certain bureaucratic routine can be established and specific divisions of the administration will become responsible. So it is understandable that this is the kind of solution they go for.

We should not dismiss planners as stupid and naive. But their training and the tradition of administration are still emphatically modernist and neither they nor we, the academics, really know how to regulate a postindustrial city that generates much more social inequality and diversity.

So is it not possible to do justice to the potential of this sort of site in a bureaucratic framework?

There is no unequivocal answer in which a particular procedure can be put forward. It is a struggle of conflicting interests—not only opposing class or social interests but also opposing interests based on particular positions which, in Gramsci's words, try to reinforce or contest the existing hegemony. The city's administrators are part of this struggle. They can call upon two elements in order to maintain this hegemony: coercion and consent. The more consent you receive from those involved, the less coercion you have to exercise. On the other hand, you have the social actors, individuals, small groups, and particular interest groups that have a different view or want to introduce different practices. They may develop a counterforce, which results in a complex interaction. There may be different positions at play. There may also be an equivalence of different positions that allow for an integrated vision.

What do we see now in the case of Tempelhofer Feld? Precisely because of the indeterminate nature of the space, a spatial structure that offers a certain stability is becoming a very important means of coercion.

So there are various possible power balances in certain spaces, which may even be institutionally acceptable. Every space has its own system of rules with particular degrees of freedom. In the case of an unused space, according to the prevailing hegemony it would have to be institutionalized in its entirety. It has to be given a purpose, and so a conflict arises between mental maps, plans, projects, and practices that are as yet nonexistent. But also between people who demand involvement by actually establishing themselves there and making it a place with a specific function, even if it is not entirely regulated. That leads to the question, Who wins? Who ultimately succeeds in simplifying that complexity and multiplicity? Because in the end it will become "something."

Is there more openness toward giving a chance to original programs and ideas than there was thirty years ago?

I think so. As I indicated, today's city no longer depends on the growth of particular sectors or on the industrial model. There is a cultivated middle class that is looking for new ways of flourishing in the city and is willing to make an effort to achieve it. Immigrants and newcomers feel more connected to their city than, for example, to their country of arrival.

We also see that the dominant view of democracy—representative democracy—is beginning to break down, and from observation we have noted that another concept is emerging under the influence of the complexity of today's society. The social concerns are so complex and so changeable that the citizen has to be consulted regularly in between elections. Coproductive planning processes have to be developed. However, this turns out not to be simple, because few people have been trained for this sort of management and mediation function. Everyone has a certain technical expertise that is employed sequentially without any coordination. Urban management, mediation, and guidance are the new tasks whose complexity is still not fully understood. For example, in the projects for the renewal of Flemish towns and cities, it says that participatory processes must be part of the course of the project, but this turns out to consist of no more than some minimal communication, a leaflet, and a hearing. It is a very difficult matter to truly involve people in the task of structuring.

In addition, we see that the role of the so-called "countermovement" has also evolved. In the past, their role was to demand that the government, which continued to retain its position of power, do things better. It was a struggle in which demands had to be agreed to. Knowledge and expertise are now more widespread, and urban movements tend to have their own professional support and do produce sound alternatives.

When you develop a more balanced power relationship, you can get more done, and that is what should happen at Tempelhofer Feld. The role of the intermediary is not to be underestimated here: just think of the architectural think-and-do tank Architecture Workroom Brussels, which mediates between the various interested parties and the authorities.

But I am in favor of developing a prior phase in which no official authority is yet involved, and the citizen or user is independent of any restriction. Citizens' initiatives, protest actions, neighborhood committees, and cultural or artistic projects are channels by which citizens can express their social concerns from the bottom up. Through these channels, every citizen can be involved in the formation of society, in the sense that he or she can help direct social developments and thus help exert influence on the organization of space. Alternative versions, which these actions may bring to the surface, may then be tested for their qualitative, technical, and aesthetic feasibility. In the social debate, you can then in many cases overcome routine and bureaucracy because you yourself are able to formulate a proposal and can put forward a contextualized plan that takes account of the huge range of variables.

Berlin is focusing on generating short-term income through tourism and is covering the costs by cooperating with property developers. How, as an action group, can one show the city authorities that the site would be more useful if it were handled in a different way?

You need powerful arguments to propose a better option in the context of the prevailing neoliberal hegemony. You could postulate different standards, such as air quality or creativity, and not just economic yield. But you will have to have a strong discourse.

Property developers are not planners, they are *betonboeren* (literally "farmers of concrete"). It's like the new Uplace shopping center a developer wants to build on the outskirts of Brussels. Those who promote that plan are not necessarily interested in whether it is commercially viable. They want to build and then they can sell it and pass it on. It is the buyer who will be left to pick up the pieces if it doesn't work.

Are there arguments for saying that Tempelhofer Feld functions perfectly in its present state?

If we extend our ideas in the context of conflict tactics, it is my opinion that it is pure fantasy to say that Tempelhofer Feld can develop to the fullest by leaving it as it is now. The temporary practice might contain a design element whereby one not only looks at what one considers important today but also examines, by means of workshops or experimentation, what this might mean for the future of the site. One cannot escape the fact that Tempelhofer Feld will be designed in a particular way. The thing is to participate in the shaping, planning, and design processes.

If activities arise out of temporary actions, you get the sort of movement that can be institutionalized. Temporary use and innovation also have a socially educational function. Temporary use can act as a sort of mini-laboratory. However, the intention is not to tackle the whole city in this sort of way but to incorporate the innovation into the standard planning. This innovation can outgrow the temporary elements. But I place high demands on those who engage in action: Do you see yourself as a vanguard, doing things that can be made more general, or do you just want to do your own thing? Creation—and especially artistic creation—can only come about by demanding an extremely egocentric freedom. But then there have to be others who can and want to recognize this creativity and make it more general.

I think that the power of a design increases when you put it in the context of actual practice. And for that you need experts and the guidance of professional designers. Take, for example, the struggle over Flagey Square in Brussels. It was won over by the synergy between a neighborhood committee, the action groups, the La Cambre architectural college, and Disturb (a network of critical designers and architects), who all backed the countermovement and thereby generated a better quality of expertise than the designers that the regional authorities had engaged. The debate on the project became a social question and not just an administrative one.

What concrete form could this take in the case of Tempelhofer Feld?

Perhaps by opting for a programmatic rather than a planning-based approach. The city authorities have made the site largely self-regulating, having left it the necessary room to evolve and intervene when conflicts flare up. The next step is for architects, planners, and spatial designers to examine its characteristics so as to keep it as open as possible and to give it as little visible structure as possible.

Can that sort of program become permanent? A constant temporary situation whose use is determined by its users?

Society does not consist of drawing up permanent collective agendas that can be revised every day. Structuring implies a certain type of sustainability. When you talk about structuring, you are talking about power relationships, because structures determine the measure of freedom that exists tomorrow.

What about the term "self-organization"? You cannot have models of self-organization that introduce everything at the same time and are in a constant temporary state. I agree that you need space for the development of creativity and for unforeseen activities. But even that space is structured and needs some planning. The resistance to the existing planning is justified, but that means that you have to think up an alternative program, with structuring that can be more pliable, flexible, and open to revision. This is an interesting starting point for experts and planners.

At Tempelhofer Feld, the undefined is important, but this cannot be designed. It is a very interesting, practical, and philosophical question, but you cannot design "emergence," because once you have designed it, it already exists. By contrast, the context can be created. A structure can be offered in which emergence is not only possible but even becomes obligatory.

In the meantime, new marginal spaces are presenting themselves where there are different power balances and where other things suddenly become possible. In this way, temporary spaces move throughout the city. Creativity often occurs in a particular context of marginality. I don't think it would be so bad if in ten years' time Tempelhofer Feld no longer appears as it does now. As long as a new Tempelhofer Feld can arise somewhere else.

But Tempelhofer Feld must be maintained as an interesting place.

That's true. But you also have to have that sort of quality control in traditional projects too. In most cases you have relatively high-quality answers in the master plan and in the visionary developments. The problem is that the monitoring of this quality weakens as the project progresses. In the first phase, everyone thinks in terms of ideal images. Problems usually only arise in the practical stages. At that point, checks have to be carried out and guidance given until the end of the process. Look at architect Renaat Braem's plans and his *Cité Modèle*. I am not in favor of that and I am not an emphatic modernist, but Braem also planned for shops, a school, a sports hall, and so on. In the end, these functions were not implemented. So you end up with a residential area comprising nothing but flats, empty car parks, and a cultural center without any staff. Is this a lack of vision or is it a lack of quality control that continues until the end of the ride? This is a very important aspect of urban planning. It is about perseverance and the will to achieve quality.

A Low-Definition Temple

LIEVEN DE CAUTER

July 2013, Brussels

In July 2013, we met with Lieven De Cauter and discussed the case of Tempelhofer Feld, especially in relation to the notion of the commons. Continuing his thoughts, he wrote the essay "Common Places: Preliminary Notes on the (Spatial) Commons" a few months later. The following text combines fragments of this essay with quotes from our conversation.[1]

The transcription of our conversation often stays close to De Cauter's exact words in order to simulate his thought process. The fragments and quotes function individually. They circle around a common theme but do not necessarily follow a linear train of thought.

1 The essay can be read in its entirety on the website of the online newspaper *DeWereldMorgen*, accessed 11 July, 2015, http://community.dewereldmorgen.be/blogs/lievendecauter/2013/10/14/common-places-preliminary-notes-spatial-commons.

The selected fragments have been copyedited, and certain corrections have been made. In some cases, they may, therefore, differ from the text in the original essay.

LIEVEN DE CAUTER:

Tempelhofer Feld is a gift that should not be thrown away. It remains an experiment, a sort of park, a sort of ... let's call it a "common," because everyone can do their own thing there.

FRAGMENT OF "Common Places: Preliminary Notes on the (Spatial) Commons"

Especially in relation to space, we are used to thinking in terms of public versus private: a space is either public or private. If we find a space that does not fit this dichotomy, we call it semi-public or semi-private. But the common is a third category. But what is this forgotten third category that we are rediscovering after it had been almost completely forgotten? If we look for the most commonplace definition of the common, it could sound like this: "The common is what is neither public (state-owned) nor private."

Tempelhof is not public space. You can't simply do carpentry work or windsurf in a public space. These activities require very specific places.

Tempelhofer Feld is a sort of gigantic hole in the city, a sea. One could call it the Tempelhof Sea. Its users feel that Tempelhof belongs solely to them and to no one else, and it thus belongs to everyone. That's the definition of a common. Why is air common? The answer is because it belongs to no one in particular and at the same time to everyone. Likewise language belongs to no one and thus to everyone. It can only belong to everyone if it in fact belongs to no one. We generally say that public space belongs to the state. Even though the state represents the citizen, there is nevertheless a difference in this nuance. Ultimately, if it were common land, the police could not take action there. It would be a domain where everyone is equal, something like a piece of unspoiled nature.

With the disappearance of nomadic culture (let's not think of it as a natural process: think wars, colonization, genocide), the commons shrink, becoming more and more a residual zone, land that is often arid or at least non-arable. From 1500 onwards the common in Europe became a reserve, like the reserves for the nomadic Native Americans in the US and Canada. This idea of the common as "protected" and imprisoned in reserves is something to stress. Of course the oceans are still common, like the air, but the North Pole is, as we write this, under threat of exploitation, as states and multinationals seek to appropriate and exploit it.

We can think of Rousseau's proto-anthropology of *le bon sauvage* (the noble savage): it is when somebody was audacious enough to fence off a patch of land and say, "this is mine," and found people stupid enough to believe him, that private property and thus inequality and, after that, regulated society had started. … It is a respect or gratefulness that we have lost. In nomadic culture you *use* nature, but you don't *own* it.

The first commonplace, the commonplace of commonplaces, so to speak, would be that nature is common. Indeed, nature is common by essence. It is the ultimate common. It is that which we share: the cosmos, the blue planet. Not only is it shared with all other humans but with all living and inanimate creatures, organic and inorganic matter. This once vast and overwhelming wholeness in which the human species one day appeared in prehistory is now a fragile and awfully limited ecosystem.

A world revolution would be needed to save Tempelhof! (laughs) That's the problem. But you could also tackle it the way the citizens' initiative stRaten-generaal have. They have changed the world a little bit by getting the Lange Wapper bridge discarded and by moving past the Flemish Government. That is a form of urban activism that one can be proud of. This group of citizens, consisting of architects, urban planners, and others, is so specialized that it simply generated a better discourse. They stopped a gigantic project that was all set: a bridge over Antwerp to close the ring road. It was a question of billions. They finished it off. Knocked it out.

If a group were to appear now—such as in the style of stRaten-generaal—and if they had enough critical power in terms of their wealth of studies and the strength of their argument, and also if they could create sufficient support by means of a referendum as, for example, stRaten-generaal did in Antwerp ... There you are, you've got it: any government can then be beaten.

DEBOOSERE / DE RAEVE:

A citizens' action group called 100% Tempelhofer Feld is currently active. They want to keep the space the way it is.

OK, it exists. Fantastic!

In that sense, as from the very first moment of this conversation, I thought in concrete terms that there at Tempelhof itself, that's where you have to act, within the boundaries of that site. By setting to work with a powerful discourse, you are involved in democracy, you are engaged in the life of a world city and you are creating a precedent. I can tell you how it should be done thanks to the work of stRaten-generaal. The Flemish Government was not happy, I can assure you of that. (laughs)

But can a referendum really change things? The plans for Tempelhofer Feld would appear to be all settled.

That is, of course, the best thing they can do. Smother all opposition even before it can get started. Simply by saying, "Don't even try, it's hopeless." It's a form of intimidation. You must not give in, you must simply beat them. One of my favorite phrases is "If you can't join them, beat them."

Is it all a matter of setting up a good marketing strategy?

There you have it: marketing. What that means is that, in your attempt to save Tempelhof, you will focus the attention of the whole city on it. Aha, that's where we need to be! Restaurants and that sort of thing, artists, intellectuals, and predictably the rich too will start saying, "Wow, Tempelhof, that's where it's all happening." In a certain sense, they will facilitate the gentrification of Tempelhof. It will become hip. All Berliners will opt for Tempelhof. Every Berliner will be proud to be able to walk across it. It will get quite busy there! (laughs)

If you defend it (by mobilizing Berlin, like 100% Tempelhofer Feld is trying to do), it will mean a gentrification of the neighborhood anyhow, because you will draw attention to something that should just be there.

That book you are going to publish focuses attention on Tempelhof too. It is part of the machinery we just saw coming into motion concerning Tempelhof. You are part of the problem. (Lieven De Cauter puts on a robot voice) "Please exterminate yourself now. Please ... ex-ter-minate ... yourself ... now!"

So let's just have a world revolution anyway, and Tempelhof will definitely be saved.

A world revolution? Is that the only possibility?

Well no, so yes, undoubtedly. We are in a neoliberal phase. Selling off the state has been going on for years. To fill the treasure chest, they have to empty the treasure. The state grows poorer everyday. This gets forgotten. We are growing poorer.

Electrabel owns our nuclear power stations.[2] They are no longer ours, but they used to be ours. That's the simple truth. We paid for the nuclear power stations and sold them for peanuts, and now Electrabel is making a huge profit. How is that possible? Obviously they didn't have to make any investment. It's simply ridiculous. The socialization of costs and privatization of the profits—it is the same routine always and everywhere. In this respect, I have become a true pupil of Marx.

You certainly don't have to convince me that neoliberalism can destroy everything. Universities, cities, museums ... they are all becoming businesses. This logic remains omnipresent. It is an extreme form of capitalism whose aim is to commodify and to privatize everything. We have to fight this with everything we have, but we are not going about it the right way. Whether it's public transport or universities, you can make endless lists. Everything is being privatized. Anything that can be privatized is privatized. Think of the genetic manipulation of potatoes, for example. It's plainly criminal and utterly absurd. Of course, we don't know which way to turn first. Shopping malls, Iraq, ecology, the North Pole, prisons—it is all being privatized. The North Pole!

2 "When the first Belgian nuclear reactors were connected to the network, the state-owned Electrabel company had a virtual monopoly on the production and sale of electricity in Belgium. As a result, it was able to impose high energy prices from 1970 on, allowing consumers to pay off the expensive nuclear power stations fast in a period of twenty years. When the European energy market was liberalized (in Flanders from 2003, in Wallonia and Brussels from 2007), a strict separation was imposed between the production, transmission, distribution, and supply of electricity. The monopoly on the supply was—at least in theory—lifted. In practice, Electrabel remained in a very privileged position. All families were automatically customers of Electrabel. In addition, Electrabel nuclear power stations were fully paid for by the citizens, and therefore it was very cheap power produced by the operator." Greenpeace Belgium, "Het ware gelaat van Electrabel," accessed June 26, 2015, http://www.greenpeace.org/belgium/global/belgium/report/2012/briefing_outofnukes_nl_def.pdf.

Doesn't the awareness of all these issues have a paralyzing effect? Don't you soon get the feeling that you can't do anything about it?

I have never understood that idea. When I disagree with something, I just go and protest. End of story. We have to understand that saying no, and really saying it as loud as possible, is a political act in itself—in and of itself. When people tell me that protesting achieves nothing, no, no, no, protesting is already something. Imagine the opposite. Something horrible happens and nobody protests. To me, protest is an aim in and of itself. Of course, you have to hope that you can defeat something, otherwise the protest is futile. The comedian Groucho Marx expressed this in a striking way: "Whatever it is, I'm against it." You can say that about anything. You have to make choices.

The question is actually, "How can I defend the wasteland that is Tempelhofer Feld, a gigantic empty lot?"

The spatial common is difficult, temporary, more a moment than a space (a moment of space). More a use than a property. It has vanished, been appropriated (for which read: has mostly been stolen) with the colonization of the territory by big farmers, the state, multinationals, etc. As we are all becoming nomads in some way or another: migrant, commuter, refugee, global student, business class, etc., but also digital nomads, internauts, cyber shepherds, etc. — the human herds a tweeting swarm — we might have to reconsider the commons. We should maximize the common: open-source knowledge (Wikipedia is a classic example, the largest and most used encyclopedia ever) will be crucial against the ongoing privatization of knowledge and research.

Tempelhof is a very interesting case. All the problems are local, but at the same time global. The interaction between the local aspect and the broader framework in which Tempelhof is situated is extremely interesting. The fact is that you are fighting for a big football field, but suddenly come face-to-face with unrestrained capitalism. This seems logical, especially in a global city such as Berlin.

Stopping a new shopping center like Uplace in Brussels is not paradoxical. By contrast, curbing the rage to build on Tempelhof ... There is an analogous paradox in our book *Art and Activism in the Age of Globalization* (NAI Publishers, 2011, coedited by Ruben De Roo and Karel Vanhaesebrouck). In the article "The Need for Free-zones: Informal Actors Setting the Urban Agenda," Eric Corijn describes how the historical station building on Luxemburgplein, which closes off and crowns the whole square, right in front of the colossus of the European Parliament, was saved (hoorah!) by the urban activist organization Citymine(d). But today the station houses the Belgian Press Centre. So what was actually saved? Perhaps the station house's facade on Luxemburgplein and a few of its ceilings? I'm glad it's there because otherwise there would be a gap. The square remains a fine place. Bravo for Citymine(d)! But this is not what they wanted to achieve. It is surely not what one dreams of as a link between Europe and the city of Brussels. It has been swallowed up into the newly constructed complex from which it was saved. The same goes for saving the Hotel Central in the very center of Brussels; we won, this beautiful city block was saved, but now it is a Marriott Hotel!

It seems to be a devilish, cast-iron law that urban activism leads to gentrification. But, at the same time, architecture is patient, and who knows, perhaps this city block will be used in new ways in a distant future. Which explains my next proposal: a heterotopia.

We don't find that of so much interest, because you then create an island in the city.

Well, I don't know. I am very fond of the notion of heterotopia. This term has not yet been used and it's worth taking a closer look at it. Tempelhof is in any case undefined. It is characterized by fuzziness, vagueness, and low definition. The other place, the place for the other, like the beach, the park, the brothel, the cinema, the museum, and so on. They are all incredibly important in a city. The temple, the cemetery, the theatre, these are more examples. Places where everything is different. Do they make the city better? Yes of course!

Some heterotopias are specialized spaces, safe havens, for this sharing of the (un)common, this common uncommon. ... This zone where nature and culture meet is one of the important mediating functions of heterotopia.

A heterotopia represents a certain value and, alas, capital too. And that is troublesome. Look at the evolution of Antwerp South. The construction of the Museum of Contemporary Art changed the entire neighborhood. It's very unfortunate for the people who lived there, but that neighborhood really was dying out. The building stock was sooner or later going to fall apart. Now it's got its shine back. I have become somewhat philosophical in that regard. The city has to last longer than that one generation that lives its life there.

Capitalism is very stubborn, of course, and again we are living in a highly liberal phase, which once again is very greedy. But, in fact, that has always been so. Capitalism is a system we have lived under for five hundred years. I am against capitalism, it is socially intolerable and so on. That's for sure, but it is there. The idea the Marxists have, of having a quick revolution and then they are rid of it, this does not work. So, what's next? The system has never simply been changed just like that. Even beheading a king is something different from changing a whole economic system.

I would be happy to give the recipe for a world revolution, but no one has a model for what should come after this revolution. Sorry. A planned economy? A zero economy? We are working on it, sir. It's easy to say "zero-growth economy" or the "self-organization of the multitude," or the "bottom-up governing of the commons." I'm all for it, but how would it work in reality?

Redistribution? Isn't that already a step in the right direction?

I am in favor of a world welfare state. It's the only solution that you could look at and say, yes, that works. The concept of the welfare state came into being in about 1949—we can study it, and there are names and systems for it. We know how it can work, and for the time being we are still living in a welfare state in Europe. It's true that the class gap is getting bigger, but most of us can still make use of unemployment benefits, family allowance, health insurance, free primary and secondary education, roads and railways, etc. But of course you are in a capitalist system.

The welfare state: at the moment we have nothing better. I simply don't see Agamben's model of anarchism working (or Negri's, or Virno's, or whoever's). Everything's on an informal basis and we just muddle along? No thank you!

The rise of capitalism has been marked in an almost allegorical, but also very real way (as documented by Marx in chapter 24 of *Capital* and by Linebaugh in his *The Magna Carta Manifesto*) by the enclosure of the common; one can say that over the past five centuries capitalism has erased the common, both its reality and even the very idea of it, and, especially in spatial terms, we do not think in terms of the commons anymore. A massive appropriation of the common has happened from two sides: the rise of capitalism has privatized the common and the rise of the (modern) state has nationalized the common: all land that is not privately owned is almost by definition state-owned. So it is not only capitalism that erased the common but also communism: everything was nationalized. So both capitalism and communism destroy or annihilate, abolish the category of the common. ... Both nature and culture are destroyed by totalitarianism, and capitalism in its totalizing phase (neoliberalism) has pretty much the same result.

(Lieven writes the following sentence down) "Is it a good idea to allow political meetings on Tempelhofer Feld?" In my view it would not be a good idea. Why? Precisely in order to preserve its political neutrality. Otherwise the Greens, or Die Linke (The Left) or any other political party, will appropriate it, and then the strength of Tempelhof will crumble. Anyone who comes to Tempelhof should come as an individual person.

Protests? No, and no Greenpeace either. Why? The answer is that it doesn't belong to anyone, but to everyone. So it's ours. So anyone who wants to fight for Tempelhof represents a single person. But take care. That's a dangerous strategy. That was the weakness of the Indignados. They wanted to remain independent of existing organizations such as the trade unions and other citizen's movements. Everyone was welcome, but only as an individual. Who represented them? Those who took part in carving out the current iteration of the space. That is radical democracy. Thus there is only one solution: consensus. That's the common and the real common. The power is no one's and is thus everyone's. One voice, and so long as one person says no we have not yet reached our goal. Everyone has to agree. That's how special of a space Tempelhof is.

It is a literal interpretation of the common, where you can do anything or nothing. All you can do there is ... just to be. You can let your sheep graze there, gather wood, but you can't live or build there. "I am making use of it, but it's not mine." I find that fascinating and that can be found at Tempelhof. I can't name any other site quite like it, apart from a real wasteland and the accompanying ecology of the drifter, the mushroom-gatherer, and the lovers in the long grass.

It is useful to once more remind ourselves of the distinction between the three spheres: the political (public) sphere, the economic (private) sphere, and the cultural sphere (as the common). There are three forms of utopia: the metastasis of politics/public — the private and the common are swallowed up by the public/political sphere, the state. This is the totalitarian utopia. Then there is the capitalist utopia (neoliberalism is utopian, as clearly shown by Hans Achterhuis): the public and the common are swallowed by the private, the economization of everything as the ultimate solution. And then there is the heterotopian utopia: a cultural institution becomes the paradigm and swallows the public (political) and the private (economic). The best known is the theocratic utopia, and these days it is rampant in all forms of religious fundamentalism, political Islam or Islamism being only its most visible form.

The common is the most elusive category of all. I support its defense. There are some very clear examples. The North Pole is common. For crying out loud! It belongs to no one, it is too important. Keep your hands off! But in a city things are different. If you think of Amsterdam's white bicycles, they were common, they belonged to everyone and to no one. But that didn't last long. So the idea of the common as self-sustaining is ... difficult. An interesting aspect is that, within the politics of the common, there is actually no decision-making body. No one can decide which words form part of the Dutch language and which do not. We decide. Next year a couple of words will be incorporated into Dutch. Why? Because we use them. The "dictionary people" have to follow what we say. No one decides what happens to the Dutch language. You can steer it very slightly in a particular direction, but what it comes down to is that the common is incredibly exciting, especially in spatial terms. We don't know what it is.

Because Tempelhof is nothing, you have to try to preserve that "almost nothingness" by making it a place of negation, a sort of cut-out. The word "temple" is related to the Greek *temenos*, which means a "cutting out." It was the place reserved for worshipping the gods. So there it is. My argument is, make it into a sort of low-definition temple, a sort of "nothing," and that is precisely its magic. Tempelhof is a pure cutout and in that sense it is also a unique temenos.

During our long conversations on heterotopia for our book *Heterotopia and the City* (Routledge, 2008), architect and coeditor Michiel Dehaene told me about the city of Karachi in Pakistan, where the cutouts of the cricket fields are very clearly defined, and remarkably enough everyone respects them. The whole city is rampant, nothing can stop that, but the cricket fields remain safeguarded. But in the case of Tempelhofer Feld you don't even have a cricket field. That's the whole puzzle. It is nothing. So, in my opinion, you have to stake a huge amount on the idea of a common. In my view, that is also what is actually going on at the moment, and what you are documenting is precisely that. The magical thing that is simply happening there is that it belongs to no one and to everyone, and that everyone then does their own thing. That's really fantastic and at the same time highly political, because it is almost a utopia. That's where it starts to become exciting. Agamben and Negri try to politicize that fantastic idea of the common, although even for them it is almost mystical. But that's what you must not do: mystify it or politicize it! Just as you should not politicize language, (Lieven shouts) LANGUAGE MUST NOT BE POLITICIZED. Only fascists or totalitarians do things like that, so that you can only say things that they deem utterable. That's simply wrong. The common must not be politicized.

The common of Tempelhof is just a temporary mirage. In a sedentary culture like ours you could nationalize all the land, while people can only own buildings. That is in itself already very utopian (for the time being at least and for the foreseeable future), but even if this could be achieved, it would still mean that the common is national, and therefore not common.

But how do you defend the common? It cannot be defended. It is a sort of holy place. "This is where it stops." As I see it, that's the key to the whole thing. That is what you have to defend, but it's hard to express it. If you had to go and explain to your average Berliner that you have discovered that this is the essence of that place ... "The essence of the place is that in fact it has no essence." (Lieven in character) "Thank you very much, sir." "Will you hang that from your window?" "No, sir."

And yet, Tempelhof seems to be able to give an idea of the common as utopia. A utopia achieved—informally—for everybody but belonging to nobody. Heterotopia ... a feeling of everything, like at the seaside or in the desert. Something almost cosmic, a gigantic void, a crater, a vastness of possibility, simply free space. But state owned. Open from 8 am to 10 pm. A tamed, and soon to be theme-parked common.

Contested Space

ANDREJ HOLM

June and September 2013, Berlin

DEBOOSERE / DE RAEVE:

Could you situate Tempelhofer Feld in Berlin's socioeconomic context?

Berlin was mainly an industrial city until the end of the 1980s. The conditions of the GDR in the eastern part and the subsidy system in the western part maintained a climate of old industrial structures. This system dissolved with reunification.[1] Most industries were shut down very quickly, because they could not keep up with international competition without these conditions. This led to an enormous rise in unemployment in both East and West Berlin. Even now, Berlin remains the German metropolis with the highest number of unemployed people.[2] Germany, one of the richest and most powerful countries in the EU, has, relatively speaking, the poorest capital. However, this goes unmentioned in all the international and political debates about Berlin. The media is mainly concerned with newfangled tourism, housing markets, and attracting the new creative class to the city.

More or less since 2008, there have been a rising number of investors moving into the city. Many real-estate funds changed ownership, and investors spent huge amounts of money to access Berlin's housing market, which consequently rocketed sky high, especially in inner-city neighborhoods. Between 2007 and 2009, for the first time in a long while, the number of people moving into the city exceeded the number of people moving out. There has been a rising demand for housing, but only a very small number of new houses have been built in the last years.

The fact that Berlin is one of the poorest cities in Germany is one of the main reasons behind the invasion of investors and new ownership structures, the immigration of the creative class, and the rising rents in inner-city neighborhoods. These are all to the detriment of

1 "Selling former GDR industrial enterprises to West German and other Western European companies induced a rapid de-industrialisation process in East Berlin. At the same time, West Berlin's excessively subsidised industries and outdated economic structure collapsed when state support was discontinued. This de-industrialisation and transformation process led to the loss of half a million factory jobs that have only partially been replaced by service and creative industries." Sabina Uffer, "The Uneven Development of Berlin's Housing Provision" (PhD diss., London School of Economics and Political Science, 2011).

a very large number of poor people. Of course, this is not comparable to poverty in Third World countries, but in the context of wealthy Germany, many of these people are now confronted with rising rents that they cannot afford. For a long time, in both parts of Berlin, the poor lived in the inner-city neighborhoods. This is in contrast to many other European metropolises, such as Paris, where affluent people have lived in the center since the 1980s, while the impoverished lived in the banlieue. Comparing a map of Berlin's increasing rents with a map of its poor neighborhoods, it is very noticeable that, over the last five years, the most deprived areas—in a social sense—are those with the highest rate of rent increase. This is why the debate on the housing issue is so contested in the public discourse. Today, most urban-related discussions are linked to the question of housing and gentrification.

Tempelhofer Feld can be seen as exemplifying this conflict. It is located in the midst of these poorer neighborhoods, where the process of deindustrialization that occurred in the 1990s is visible, and the pressure on the housing market is marked. The housing question plays a major role in articulating and legitimizing strategies for the development of the former airfield, especially according to the Senate. Planners argue that Berlin needs accommodation to solve the housing question, although I would say it's obvious that three or four new apartment blocks on Tempelhofer Feld will never solve the problem of Berlin's housing shortage.

I would add that in discussing arguments for and against its development, it is also more meaningful to situate the debate on Tempelhofer Feld within a broader Berlin context than to try and understand different actors' positions on a microscale. Conversely, it makes sense

2 In 2013 a total of 210,093 people were unemployed in Berlin, which corresponds to 11.7% of the city's employable population. Statistik Berlin Brandenburg, accessed June 18, 2015, http://www.statistik-berlin-brandenburg.de/.

People who are registered in the welfare system can accept a so-called *Minijob* to supplement their income to a livable amount. While they stay supported by the state, they no longer count as unemployed in the statistics. People taking part in the job agency's obligatory training courses are also not counted as unemployed. "FAQ für Einstiegsseite Statistik im Internet," accessed June 18, 2015, http://statistik.arbeits-agentur.de/Statischer-Content/Alternative-Startseite/FAQ-Statistik.pdf.

to focus on a single point in a conflict about urban development, in this case Tempelhofer Feld, to better understand the city as a whole.

What might an analysis of the Tempelhofer Feld conflict reveal?

There are undoubtedly a lot of strategies at play in this conflict. These strategies can be linked to the many different interest groups that lay claim to Tempelhofer Feld. It makes sense to see the field as a focus of conflict, of contested urbanism. Everybody is trying to use this space for his or her own ends, and it is not easy to understand this at first glance. If you understand that people use it as an instrument, it immediately raises questions about what their interests are. This is what sociologist Manuel Castells says, "Do not try to understand the movement or the conflict for itself, but use the conflict to understand the structure that lies underneath."

Does the temporary state of Tempelhofer Feld provide a speculative value for real-estate agencies and governmental structures?

It could have a direct effect on the real-estate value for the streets that share a view of the field, but it remains limited to an area of perhaps a hundred meters around the field. I don't believe that it's possible to really change a neighborhood by simply modifying the conditions of the structure alone. It does not change because an old industry or a harbor closes, a stadium is built or in this case an airport is shut down. This change is set in motion much earlier.

It is important to understand that there is not a whole, unified block of politicians in the government that share a common interest. If you analyze all the propositions and activities surrounding Tempelhofer Feld, you will discover that a lot of different parts of the administration have their own vested interests and that they are competing amongst themselves. This means that within the government there are conflicts and arguments. These conflicts do not arise because Tempelhofer Feld is so important for Berlin; the field is mainly deployed as a tool when conflicts arise.

Initially, it was not the Senate's idea to open the whole field. They changed their strategies and their way of viewing the space and integrated physical and social activities with the creativity of Berlin. The participatory elements they introduced are the same strategies that real-estate investors use. They try to use the spontaneous activities of the people to enforce their own strategies and to put their own interests in a better light. Of course, this is not only a process of give and take, it is contested and bargained for in a way that is not easy to analyze. It's a battle in which you also have alliances that change.

One of the main motivations of the Berlin Senate for the development of the field is that Berlin is in desperate need of housing. You mentioned that three or four apartment buildings would never solve the housing question. But isn't the need to increase housing undeniable?

Yes, Berlin needs housing, and especially affordable housing for people with lower incomes. Today, this means housing with rents below 5.50 euro per square meter. It's obvious that new buildings will never deliver such affordable housing. Investors claim that they can meet prices of 7 euro per square meter if they are subsidized. This remains too expensive for many people. There are 400,000 households in Berlin that live below the poverty line and need affordable housing under 5.50 euro per square meter. Many need even lower rents.

These new buildings may be necessary in a quantitative sense. We have an increasing number of residents and of course they need houses. But new buildings cannot solve the housing question in a social sense. Therefore, "Berlin needs housing" is a bit of an ambiguous argument. I'd like to change the question "what does Berlin need?" to "what do people with low incomes need?" It doesn't make sense to address an abstract housing question to Berlin as a whole, when 400,000 households are left behind and have to reduce their housing standards.

The problem concerning social housing in Germany is that the state mainly deals with private interests. Subsidy programs fund private investors. The government gives a certain amount of money, and the private investors deliver affordable housing units for a limited time. After thirty years they can put them on the free market. Naturally this is completely ineffective, because it only ensures temporary social use. The problem of the housing question is not the law but the private sector's interest in generating profit. For example, it would make much more sense to transform more housing into social housing and within public ownership.

The problem lies in the fact that politicians never restrict the idea of the free-market economy itself. They swim with the market, moderating some of its effects, sometimes reducing some of those effects, or spending money to create affordable rents. But everything they do and all the money they spend eventually generates private profit. It's easy to understand that private profit and social housing are not compatible. Instead of producing private profit in order to obtain some social effect, policy should change and limit profit, in order to achieve real social change. Today, social agendas are reached by embedding them into the market and by approving their market power and producing private profit. It does not make sense that common goals should only be met by securing private profit.

What is the composition of the neighborhoods surrounding Tempelhofer Feld?

A large area of Tempelhofer Feld is in Neukölln, which is a district of primarily outdated housing stock that is generally in a bad condition. The neighborhoods around Flughafenstraße and Okerstraße are places where the majority of inhabitants are still poor, and where more than 75 percent of the families depend on social welfare. The eastern and southern sides of the field are part of the Tempelhof district, and some of its neighborhoods are very different to Neukölln. These are all buildings that were built over a long period, from the 1920s to the 1960s. All are high-rise buildings with very small housing units that do not meet twenty-first-century comfort needs. They are practical, compact, and functional. It is difficult to give these buildings a purpose other than what they were originally built for, so the social structure of its residents remains the same: traditional families, couples, and singles. This is a totally different social composition compared to that of Neukölln, which mainly consists of immigrant families. However, Tempelhof is not a wealthy neighborhood. When we look at the income of the people on the Tempelhof side of the field we see people with more or less low to lower-middle-class incomes. The proportion of children going to higher education is only slightly higher than that of Neukölln. The biggest difference is that the Tempelhof side is not attractive to expats, artist communities, cultural activists, and so on. Since there aren't spaces available to accommodate shops on the ground floor in most of the buildings, it is more difficult to transform this neighborhood into "the next place to be."

Neukölln is rapidly changing, but in a different way than the gentrification processes we have observed in Prenzlauer Berg or Friedrichshain. There was no massive investment in the physical upgrading of buildings. The gap between existing rents and the assumed rents of new contracts is very high. This means there is a huge interest in displacing tenants without any desire to invest in better housing quality. It is more profitable for investors to close the gap between the rents for current tenants and possible new contracts. In Prenzlauer Berg, shifting the population was encouraged in the process of modernizing the neighborhood. This was necessary in order for residents to accept paying more for rent. Gentrification in Prenzlauer Berg and other East Berlin neighborhoods is taking shape in this two-way process, whereby a physical upgrade is changing the social structure of its population. In Neukölln only the social structure is changing. I call this process "rental gentrification."

A second issue that distinguishes Neukölln's transformation is that it is the first district in Berlin in which gentrification is directly linked to international migration. Berlin has long-standing experience of migration from abroad, but mainly of migration from poorer countries: Eastern Europe, Yugoslavia, Spain, Portugal, and of course Turkey. This was naturally never linked to a gentrification process. Today, Berlin is attracting people who are highly educated, with high incomes, from other Western European countries and from North America. The number of these newcomers went up three or four times compared to figures from 2005.

What positive effect could the current state of Tempelhofer Feld have on its surrounding neighborhoods?

What I find interesting is that Tempelhofer Feld has the potential to be a new sort of public space, one where different parts of the neighborhood and even different neighborhoods can come together. In my opinion, it's exactly in such public spaces that it is possible for people to connect and to grasp that society consists of a wide variety of people. Neukölln is a perfect example of a social mix that doesn't work. Statistically we could call it a mixed neighborhood, but there is no mixed use of space. There are no links between different groups. Neighbors rarely share life experiences on the streets. This is much less so on Tempelhofer Feld, where links between different groups are made possible. I believe that the desire to create a free space can generate more connections between people and could therefore act as a bridge between different classes, ages, and groups of people. In that way I think it is an extraordinary space.

How do these different groups interact with each other on Tempelhofer Feld?

There is more visibility and this strengthens the notion of "the other." In these statistically mixed neighborhoods everybody stays very much in their own world, within their own networks, usually restricted to people like themselves. This is not a strategy but an effect. Within Tempelhofer Feld it is apparent that people use this space in different ways, seeing and meeting each other. I think that even just seeing others different from oneself is already a strong precondition for a subsequent discussion of what could be of a common interest. Tempelhofer Feld could function as some sort of network or platform for social mixture.

If the plans for Tempelhofer Feld were open to discussion, what would you like to add?

I think the question in this case would be to reflect on how we can empower the people who are using the space. They have to be included in the planning process. It would be interesting if it were possible to see how such a space would be developed, step by step, as people use it. This process will be stopped if formal proceedings for a classic development plan are set in motion. So many other parts of the city are already planned by the state or by private owners. The question we should be asking is not how many square meters of Tempelhofer

Feld remain green but who designs the future of this place, and following this train of thought, who designs the future of the city, our life, and our society.

Between Intention and the Unplanned

KENNY CUPERS

August 2013, Berlin

"Ideally, the public domain is that which belongs to everybody and therefore to nobody in particular. In this sense it promises us a free space unencumbered by the determinants of the private or the particular; a space which harbors the spontaneous and the unexpected; a space which brings us in touch with the enchanted world lying beyond the functional, the controlled, the intentional, and the planned. In other words, what is so great about public space is its potential degree of indeterminacy and freedom."

"Can we produce spaces that are freer in their use than the places that are conventionally built? To what extent can 'free space' be planned or designed? We can design benches and pavements, but can we install through design the indeterminacy of public life?"

"The fate and fortune of public space is not a matter either of the absence or abundance of design. It is a question of the interplay between the two — between intention and the unplanned, planning and the unexpected, routine and freedom."[1]

1 Kenny Cupers, "Promises of a Free Space," in *Openbaarheid, Cahier #3*, edited by Vlaams Bouwmeester (Brussels, 2011), 207–15.

DEBOOSERE / DE RAEVE:

Your essay "Promises of a Free Space" conveys the feeling we had when we first set foot on Tempelhofer Feld. What are the origins of your ideas about the balance between intention and the unplanned in public space?

In 2001, just after I'd graduated, I moved to Berlin where I began working for Studio Libeskind. I very quickly became disenchanted by the lack of reflection on the role of architecture in the city. I had graduated with a thesis on public space, and I noticed a great many spaces in the daily life of Berlin that weren't defined as public space but were used as such. By that I mean spaces that weren't defined by their architecture but rather by their use. That fascinated me and I wanted to research it further. I joined forces with Markus Miessen, who was also working for Libeskind at that time. That's how our book *Spaces of Uncertainty* (Verlag Müller + Busmann, 2002) came about. We looked more closely at these residual spaces and observed how they were used. Their use occurred within various kinds of time frames, and we analyzed both short-term and long-term use that contributed to the public life of the city. I spent a lot of time in these residual spaces, and that experience was one of the main starting points for the essay.

How did you develop the idea further?

The most important criticism of *Spaces of Uncertainty* is that it didn't present any agenda for architecture. Our interest in residual spaces was interpreted by many, and especially by architects, as a sort of acquiescence: "Let it happen. Architecture no longer has a role to play in urban development." For that very reason, in my essay I questioned what the role of architecture in such a context might be. Can architects or designers organize the unplanned without planning it? That's clearly a contradiction. I knew it wasn't the first time this question had been asked. So I looked at the utopian projects of the 1950s and 1960s. I wanted to know what they thought about organizing free activity in the city back then, and how that actually determined the architecture that was created. That led me not only to famous utopian projects such as Constant Nieuwenhuys's New Babylon and Cedric Price's Fun Palace, but also to less renowned such as the Animation Hall in the Centre for Fine Arts in Brussels and the cultural centers designed by Frank van Klingeren. The analysis showed that there were, in fact, real attempts to build the radical "free space" proposed by Nieuwenhuys and Price, even though these attempts were limited by compromises and sometimes had the opposite effect. This insight offers us a specific historical answer to the question of the extent to which the unplanned can be planned. Is the unplanned still just a fleeting moment in the biography of a city or society, or should we view it as a sort of universal norm to aim for? The first hypothesis seems to me to be a more workable basis for urban activism today.

The utopian approach taken by Price and Nieuwenhuys has long since been co-opted into today's capitalist urban development; the current policy on the unplanned therefore exists in an entirely different set of dynamics from that of the 1960s and 1970s. In any case, how can we possibly assess the built environment with the matrix of planned versus unplanned? Price's InterAction Centre, which was realized in London in 1976, worked, for example; but the question is when, and for whom. I don't believe in total solutions. The temporary aspect is central to such projects, but obviously time has different dimensions. We also see this when we look at raumlabor's project for Tempelhofer Feld. Their strategic development of the site was based on impermanence—first in the context of a few months, then over the course of a few years and finally for a period of twenty years. How do you evaluate such a multi-temporal plan by means of the simple antithesis of the planned versus the unplanned?

> Constant Nieuwenhuys and Cedric Price's designs started from scratch. When you start from an existing entity, as was the case with Tempelhofer Feld, it's different. It would seem logical to look at what's already there and to give it another purpose with as little adaption as possible.

I think this happens a lot in reality, especially in Berlin. Many of the places that functioned as refuges in 2001 and 2002 and which we photographed for *Spaces of Uncertainty* have now disappeared. Some places have been transformed into a classical park, other areas have made way for apartment blocks or supermarkets. The danger is that one views these refuges with nostalgia, instead of seeing them as moments in the life of a city. That's why architecture has to be very dynamic in relation to this reality instead of obstinately trying to define a refuge. I think that's where the misunderstanding arises. When you're dealing with the uncontrolled, there's a good chance that it then becomes too controlled. But conversely, there are, of course, real processes that do require more control. For example, rapidly increasing rents are a major problem in Berlin at the moment. In the last five years, in particular, this has created social tensions. Berlin needs affordable housing more than it needs parks, and that requires careful but decisive planning at the regional level.

The current, temporary situation at Tempelhofer Feld was designed. Is it true to say that this is an exceptional case?

There is certainly a fresh wind blowing through urban development in Berlin, especially if you look back at the 1990s. People like Philipp Oswalt have brought about a sort of rejuvenation of thinking. The city council understands that these temporary activities are important and may bear fruit in the long term. But in the 1970s and 1980s in New York, for example, developers gave artists free spaces with the intention of transforming them into expensive lofts at a later stage. In that sense, the instrumental use of temporary and/or artistic activities in a long-term development process is not really new. Therefore, I do think it's important that not only private developers are involved with temporary use but also the government.

In the case of Tempelhofer Feld, this impermanence has indeed been developed. There is a kind of minimal definition or framing of the site, which allows for certain activities; for the time being, there is no need to define everything in great detail. In that sense, we can state that a design may consist of very few elements, at least initially. Minimal materialization, a few fences, signposting, and that's all.

Can you elaborate on the conclusion to your essay "Promises of a Free Space"?

"Instead we need to ask, what could free space look like in real space—urban space that is a palimpsest of histories and memories, that is both the result and medium of politics and power, conflict and contestation. The nature of urban space does not preclude the existence of free spaces, but it does require an approach to design that is able to avoid the consensual and to creatively transform conflict into negotiation. In our attempts to create a more open public domain, we will need to think of indeterminacy as inherently partial. That could lead us to develop a strategically designed indeterminacy that takes into account why and for whom it is meant."[2]

This idea resulted from the analysis of utopian visions such as those of Constant Nieuwenhuys and Cedric Price. How can the abstract idea of a free, indeterminate space shape the design of concrete spaces, such as Tempelhofer Feld? It is a question to which I've given no clear answers in my conclusion. But I point in the direction of a kind of strategic "unplannedness" or the formulation of the conditions under which that dynamic can take place, and I imply that such visions can be implemented in a renewed agenda for the architect.

What's important to me is to reflect upon this dynamic practice in urban development. Not to look at the city as a string of nineteenth-century street blocks, as was the custom in the 1990s, but to see the urban fabric as a kind of field of activities and concentrations that change in the course of time, a vision that Koolhaas formulated back in the 1990s.

The spatial challenges are becoming more complex. How can the architect deal with this?

The architect perhaps may not be in the best position here, because he is affected not only by his personal motives but also by the societal role that is imposed on him, namely to produce building plans. A new figure has to emerge, one that can put this ideology of professionalism aside. Call it an urban coach or programmer or whatever—there are already various terms to describe this role. But, at heart, it is a person who offers a different kind of expertise, far more focused on the dynamics of daily life itself and not on fixing places in time in the long term. The emphasis is more on the supervision or curation of space.

2 Ibid., 215.

In fact, that is what raumlabor and Urban Catalyst studio have already proposed. The task of the new "non-architect" is therefore to establish a flexible program in time and space. I think it is more rewarding for an architect or artist to keep a dialogue going and to guide a vision, but without dodging the issue.

Film and images can play an important role in developing a critical approach to the various perceptions of Tempelhofer Feld. This may help create something that is more than just "building" and make people think about the societal role that architecture in all its dimensions can play. Then it becomes a versatile form of expertise. Of course, new architecture courses are then required, to teach more than just how to design buildings that don't leak.

But the "curating" of a city is not necessarily a magical solution either. I have to admit that I am quite critical of the fact that such an approach is often restricted to the cultural sector. There are too few sustained interventions in the proliferation of local biennials and cultural events, so I don't think that these things have much effect and get the impression they only serve a relatively small cultural elite. It is more worthwhile to dedicate oneself to a project over a longer and more intensive period rather than hopping from one pioneering project to the next.

Conflict as a Productive Mode of (Spatial) Practice

MARKUS MIESSEN

October 2014, Berlin

DEBOOSERE / DE RAEVE:

When and how did you become interested in the notion of participation, and how did you develop your view on this topic in your different publications and projects?

In about 2001, when I was working on *Spaces of Uncertainty* (Verlag Müller + Busmann, 2002) with my friend and colleague Kenny Cupers, we found ourselves becoming increasingly frustrated with the way in which architecture in general was developing. Missing the presence of the political within the architectural realm, I asked myself, How can a spatial practitioner participate in the production of urban reality—and, more generally, spatial planning on various scales—differently from his or her expected role?

From the start, I made a clear distinction between the historical perspective on participatory practices and my personal interest in participation, which was based on the question, What can I do or what do I have to do to participate in something? As an ongoing research project this idea developed across several publications. *Did Someone Say Participate? An Atlas of Spatial Practice* (MIT Press, 2006, coedited by Shumon Basar) can be seen as an overview in the sense of an anthology looking at those practices which are committed to a more critical production of space. These observations were not necessarily made in the context of architecture or urbanism per se, but within a very diverse set of practices that would have an effect on space. This eventually led to the question, What does participation mean today, and how can we argue its misinterpretation or misuse in a productive manner?

The Violence of Participation (Sternberg Press, 2007) was simultaneously a project contribution for the Lyon Biennale that resulted in a publication. The Biennale invitation was an opportunity to test some of the hypotheses set out in *Did Someone Say Participate?* These experiments and the ensuing reflections resulted in *The Nightmare of Participation* (Sternberg Press, 2010), which can be seen as my main thesis based on three considerations. The first defines the role of the "uninvited outsider," an individual or collective that wants to achieve something and therefore crafts a framework for engagement or creates a point of entry to enable them to act in a field in which they normally would not be invited to participate. The second is the deromanticization of the classical, conventional, or historical model of participation, which premises that it should be an all-inclusive, democratic model regardless of whether this actually fits a specific situation. The third presents a role model I derived from the political function of the "crossbencher" in the British House of Lords. I am further developing the concept and notion of the crossbencher in my forthcoming book, *Crossbenching*. The idea is for it to become a reflective manual on how to act in the context of a possible, but different form of participatory practice, and a rendering of an alternative regarding the forms of participation that we currently think of and refer to when talking about participation.

The subproject *Waking Up from the Nightmare of Participation* (Expodium, 2011, coedited by Nina Valerie Kolowratnik) asked a group of practitioners from different fields and backgrounds to use *The Nightmare of Participation* as a springboard to develop ideas or, alternatively, to critique it. It was meant as an inducement for discussion. I made it clear that whatever their contribution, it would be published exactly the way in which they submitted it. Part of the idea was that it would not become a "friendly" situation where everyone pats everyone else on the back, something one can find quite often in the cultural milieu that we tend to work in. This does not foster any progress or productive development.

Participation in its passive or reactionary form—when people wait for someone else to invite them to participate—is not very fruitful. This is, of course, exactly how post-labor politicians have understood the game: participation—in its traditional form—has become more of a mechanism for elected politicians to cover up or withdraw from their actual responsibility for decision-making. Of course, I am not against any kind of democratic, bottom-up, or social principle in terms of the basic understanding that everyone has the same rights. But I do not believe that design should, by necessity or default, be democratic. In fact, I do not think that design can ever be a fully democratic process. You can describe it, or sell it, as something seemingly democratic, but the outcome will in most cases be less interesting, less challenging, and less productive. I am looking for a more proactive approach to something that is propositional, and this is where the role of the designer or architect can be very interesting.

The architect as the sole creator of a vision?

No, I do not believe that designers have some sort of divine expertise. But they know how to control a specific set of tools. Even if a person has the skills to mediate or to introduce a situation to a large number of people, a consensus is needed in order to make a decision and to move one step forward. But when you have to act consensually and to consider the opinions of a large group of people, ideas will always be watered down. Within a democratic process, such as this one, every individual has the right to vote, which can also and easily lead to terrible situations and—more importantly in the context of architecture or urbanism—terrible designs and spatial results, realities that we have to live with. However, I do not support the modernist model of the architect from heaven who, in a "Frank Gehry-esque" manner, drops a design from the helicopter that is then supposed to solve our problems. I am more interested in a discourse that is productive through conflict and that explores friction as a design tool, generating new content instead of being simply self-affirmative.

What do you mean by "productive through conflict"?

When I talk about conflict as a productive mode of practice, I mean that conflict can take place in the moment of collaboration, but also in the moment in which friction between different actors and objects occurs. If you can act as an "uninvited outsider," you do not have to report to anyone. In other words, if there is no consensual framework to which you have to obey, you can explore the generative aspects of conflict.

At this point, I would also like to underline the difference between cooperation and collaboration. When people talk about collaboration within the context of a project they often, in fact, mean cooperation. This is a common misunderstanding. Many projects are not based on collaboration but cooperation—a more peer-to-peer understanding of practice; while the term collaboration has a historical connotation, meaning collaborating with the enemy in times of war or conflict. It needs to be read and understood as a temporary joint effort with an opponent in order to overcome a complex situation. Without this collaboration there would be no solution. It presents a state of exception. This is interesting, because in order to kick off a genuinely collaborative project, you need to be a free radical of sorts, attached neither to any institutional framework nor to any particular party involved.

In a formal political context, this is where the role of the "crossbencher" comes in. Although the crossbencher in the House of Lords takes his place in a most conservative and reactionary model of politics, I see potential in this as a critical analogy.[1] The role of the individual crossbencher is that of an independent politician not aligned with any (other) party within the House of Lords. The spatial arrangement of the crossbenches also reflects this: a physical object, a set of benches, set perpendicularly in the middle of the space, squeezed between the government and opposition parties.

Does this crossbencher act as an intermediary between different actors?

The question is how this intermediate role is understood and practiced. My fear is that if it is not brutally executed, the mediator will become precisely the person who facilitates consensus. If we look at your example of Tempelhofer Feld, everything that has happened there so far is a drop in the ocean. There have been many projects and propositions up to now that we will most probably not remember. This is not to belittle their efforts in any way. These projects have often been smartly critical, they manage to find resonance in a very specific milieu, which essentially is the milieu in which most of us practice and situate ourselves conceptually, discursively, and ethically. But—and this is difficult to say because I really love these kinds of

1 "The crossbench politician is essentially an independent practitioner who neither belongs to a specific party nor regularly fosters alliances with the same political camps. Although this also makes him or her a less reliable or dependable player, potentially even without a clear stance, it offers an alternative disinterested and less biased perspective toward the internal, consensus-driven mechanisms of the other political parties present in the House of Lords. Although these politicians have an undoubtedly political stance and opinion, they do not subscribe to the nailed-down membership books or party platforms of other, consolidated politicians."
Markus Miessen, *The Nightmare of Participation*, (Sternberg Press, 2011), 243.

projects—my real fear is that they actually do not work *against* what is happening on a political level but instead *endorse* it. The question instead should be how to achieve a major political decision or some form of central policy change in this regard. Considering the size and importance of Tempelhofer Feld as an urban site, these projects are mostly too small in scale and political ambition to generate enough political pressure.

For a site and project like this one, for something to really change, one would need to mobilize large numbers of people. I do not mean some sort of bottom-up or participatory approach, but the creation of major pressure so that certain decisions taken by the local government can no longer be pussyfooted around. If we look at all the large-scale projects in Berlin, this has basically been the situation for a number of years: PhD-level pussyfooting by politicians.

What do you believe should happen with a significant site like Tempelhofer Feld?

On the one hand, I certainly do not think that the entire site should just remain as it is, or that it should simply be an open romantic field. Yet its openness, of course, has certain qualities, and for that reason a substantial section should stay open and "usable," whatever this means, by a public—whatever that means. On the other hand, the general housing situation in Berlin is in a poor state, and any potential decision regarding the site should take social housing into account as well.

Given Berlin's dire financial state, Tempelhofer Feld could be a site that—with a smart strategy of cross-financing—could be turned into a fantastic inner-city refuge and at the same time something that generates money which can be used to build affordable housing in the city. Most proposals until now have ignored the real urban political problems. Berlin is generally being promoted and experienced as an attractive, not to say "cool" geography. What most of the previous proposals suggested is to try and make it even more attractive in terms of a stylized heterotopia. Well, I'm sorry to say, but Berlin has many serious problems and issues to deal with, most notably affordable housing for those who are not part of the creative community that the city government is promoting. Berlin does not need to become more alternative, but instead it needs to face reality and get its act together as a city. Berlin is now already a parody of itself.

What I really miss at a municipal level is the moment when politicians make decisions and take responsibility, not in terms of two to five years—i.e., up to the next election—but twenty to thirty years, with a clear and responsible vision. For years, local and federal politicians have been pursuing a plethora of strategies for tourism—be it creative tourism, artistic tourism, architectural tourism, or tourism in general—hoping that this would foster some sort of economically sustainable model for the future of the city. Now everyone is talking about gentrification. I don't want to listen to this anymore. I am surrounded by people writing the most critical texts and practicing the most critical projects, and who go on about gentrification and how bad it is, but of course they all live in the same area (which is where I also live) in Berlin Mitte on the border with Prenzlauer Berg, which is probably the area where gentrification has done most harm to the city. But do you think it will be different in other neighborhoods like Neukölln, Wedding, or Moabit? Of course not. The only way to stop this process is not through critical writers, who write witty essays in magazines that will be read by two hundred people, but through a political decision about affordable housing in the city center. Call me naive, but the only thing that can make this possible is money. Serious money. So the question is, how can the city of Berlin generate the money necessary to meet its needs? Tempelhofer Feld is a huge site in the city center with an amazing landscape and amazing potential in terms of infrastructure, but so far I have not seen any heterogeneous proposal that is politically realistic.

> Urban Catalyst studio and raumlabor proposed an evolutionary plan in which the site would be developed over twenty years as an experimental place for different practices. Out of these practices new economies could surface, defining the future of the site.

Yes, and I agree that out of all the proposals that I have seen this was the most viable one. This is very interesting, but still remains within the milieu in which we are comfortable. To generate real change, it would have to be something much more hard-core, something that we probably all really think of as the goddamn Antichrist. That is what I refer to when talking about collaboration. If we only go after the things we have an interest in ourselves, the situation will not change. What is needed is something that generates big bucks. In the long term, another urban gardening project or start-up will not generate enough revenue to make it work. From then on, the question is how we can we push an opportunistic idea through while creating a win-win situation rather than a consensual model.

For example, at one point there was a proposal for the media site Babelsberg to enter into a potential cooperation. The film school and a whole group of production companies would be brought to Tempelhofer Feld. Today, Babelsberg is close to Berlin, but at the same time it is not in Berlin but Potsdam. It lacks certain urban infrastructure, which makes it less appealing for international visitors. Moreover, it is not connected to companies in the city. There is a kind of physical gap. We have a one-off opportunity here, which is a huge empty lot in the middle of the city, which is unprecedented internationally. So Babelsberg would move into the city and, in a long-term strategy, turn Tempelhofer Feld into a tech park, similar to the Valley in Los Angeles. Relocating the heart of the local film industry into the particular geography of Tempelhofer Feld would create a hub with the potential for physical expansion. It could attract a lot of nestling industries that are closely connected to film production, like software companies. To be honest, it is not a subject I am interested in. Also, I think that the proposal was not fully developed. I couldn't care less whether Babelsberg is in the city or not. There may be flaws in this proposal, yes, but what is interesting is that it unfolds a relatively realistic model with growth potential over time, while allowing for parts of the site to retain its current marginal feel. Real industries would be brought to the city, which Berlin seriously lacks. At the same time, it would be soft industries in the sense that they are environmentally friendly service industries. A lot of 3D animation is done in Berlin, and the idea would be to cluster all these activities. If you could actually condense it all at one physical site, it would be a great advantage: the site as a productive machine. In this case, a cultural product or cultural industry that speaks to a slightly larger, more international audience would produce money that could be used to generate the cultural projects that were proposed for the site, and at the same time be back-channelled into the city to create large-scale housing projects that would benefit a larger constituency. This does not mean that the whole site would be turned into a film park, but certain areas could be productively exploited in that way. This, from my point of view, is a very interesting general approach to the site: on the one hand, through its financial exploitation, and on the other, through a kind of cultural gain that goes hand in hand with the idea of preserving the existing landscape, something I agree that the city should not lose, even if there is already an abundance of parks and green areas.

You are suggesting that Tempelhofer Feld also has to play a functional role by housing an industry that provides financial means for the city.

The city is like an engine. It is constantly running and it needs fuel to run on. Unfortunately—and I am not saying this from the viewpoint of some capitalist theory—money is the fuel of the city. A site like Tempelhof has a tremendous potential to become a micromachine, a mini-city. I agree, of course, with the Prician notion of the Fun Palace but a "fun palace" also needs to be financed. Anything else would be naive. Certain parts could still keep their urban, anarchic feeling, and other sections could be developed in a ruthless manner. I would be very interested in this dichotomy and what this could potentially generate. This dichotomy is also what I understand as the urban condition rather than some flatlined, homogeneous superculture. So that there is actually a kind of engine running, which produces something that the city as a whole would benefit from. There is this weird misunderstanding that the site as it is now is for everyone in Berlin, a site for the public at large. But in fact it concerns only a very specific public. The people that go there are mostly from the surrounding areas. How can the city as a whole benefit from Tempelhofer Feld? It is, from my point of view, a question of affordable social housing and other things from which people living in Berlin but participating in other milieus may benefit as well.

Isn't the government in Berlin already cooperating with private investors?

That has always been a complete farce, because it has always involved the development of cheap visions. By cheap I mean not only really inadequate in terms of architectural and urban conception but also financially cheap, that is to say "budget visions," because the city never had the funds or the clientele to appropriately investigate the possibilities. If Berlin wants to run a project like Tempelhofer Feld properly, it should put three or four million euro aside and set up a team that takes on the role of an "uninvited outsider" in order to research potentials. This team should not be connected to any party or interest group. They should be pre-radical in the sense that they should be given carte blanche to think about potentials. The group should spend three to four years preparing a substantial investigation into the capabilities of the site, its protagonists, and its potential future(s). This investigation should also be developed in a dirty direction, which means that the group should not only think in terms of intellectually stimulating cultural approaches but further in terms of something that would be realistic and financially viable in the longer term.

How do you relate this to what raumlabor and Urban Catalyst studio did? They infiltrated into the development project of the Berlin Senate and generated a budget to do further research.

They were close to the understanding of the "uninvited outsider." Only they did not manage to involve "the enemy." The budget was probably quite modest and also had to be used to create an exhibition and a publication and so on. So it ended up becoming the same kind of cultural project like so many others. The conversation mostly remained within the expected milieu and audience.

Seen in the context of the city as a whole, this approach could be upgraded, I believe. It has been a similar story with projects such as Based in Berlin, for which former mayor Klaus Wowereit invested two million euro in a large-scale show that supposedly delivered an overview of the contemporary artistic practices from a particular generation living or "based" in Berlin. But everyone already knows about the quality of production in Berlin. Also, the show did not even represent this quality. The money spent on this dreadful concept could have been used instead to create an infrastructure for artists living in Berlin or to produce studio spaces. I don't want to know who makes these decisions. In fact, I do know who makes these decisions. The problem is, what can we do about it? If you really want to make a change—and this, unfortunately, is and always needs to be a long-term ambition—you practically have to go into formal politics, and you have to take a smart approach.

So, rather than constantly talk about interdisciplinary or transdisciplinary approaches, I would push for an inter-milieu approach. Instead of combining practices that usually already work together—like an architect or urbanist working with a graphic designer, artist, or sociologist—we have to try to combine practices into what one may call a dirtier project—a form of dirty reality based on genuine collaboration. By dirty I mean against hipness. Ninety percent of the proposals that I have seen for Tempelhofer Feld were hip projects. They created an atmosphere that internationally was directly understood in a way, which is very much about the now, the moment, the current spatial-visual language and codes. It is time to acknowledge the fact that Berlin is a city rather than a village, and a city is a complicated and, by default, a conflictual structure with huge numbers of constituencies that often do not have the same interests.

Urban Catalyst studio and raumlabor tried to push their ideas through but in the end their plans were only partly executed. What could they have done to reach a different outcome?

It is a very easy calculation. Politicians are only interested in two things: the first being that the developed project works—i.e., that the project will be a success—and the second, that it generates revenue. The question of revenue is not necessarily a negative one in regard to some kind of auto-exploitation of the city but instead should be seen as a capital potential. Where most of the interesting proposals probably failed was in the formation of a collaborative team, a group of heterogeneous decision-makers with someone smart in a position to take the lead. I am aware that this takes time and effort, so in that regard I am not blaming anyone. It cannot be expected of anyone to do this work for free or in a precarious setup. But I still have not seen a single proposal that tried to integrate major developers or industries into the cultural substrata in order to create ideas and a working vision together.

To accept a plan as credible, the city needs security in terms of investment. This investment is not going to come from cultural institutions, neighborhood groups, interesting curators, artists, or architects. I am talking about real investors, people that will bring in the money. So to create a dirty project means to work with people you usually would not like to work with. Of course, this is a terrible job and a real challenge. But it needs to be done. Berlin in its current state of affairs and cultural politics is not only exploiting itself but also cannibalizing itself.

The tricky question would be how the model of dirty collaboration could become a test case for the use of a different and more responsible form of cultural production and, to put it in popular terms, the development of a win-win situation. I think there should be a vision of how certain goals for "the public at large" could be achieved, not simply for "a public." There should be a framework designed to accomplish such a vision, and there should be an allocation of roles.

This needs to be understood as any kind of process that sets up a framework. Interviews should select qualified people for the job and bring together different actors. Possibly some of them will hate each other from the beginning. The casting process itself, when someone leads it with relative freedom, could actually turn the "bound-to-be-conflictual" situation into something productive. What is important is not the structural mechanism that enables as many people as possible to participate in a project but participation in and development of content, and the way that this content and investment can possibly change the reality of the city.

A New Ambition

ROELAND DUDAL

August 2013, Berlin

DEBOOSERE / DE RAEVE:

The theme of the project *The Ambition of the Territory* includes the ongoing discussion on the further expansion of the urban system at the cost of the limited number of open spaces that remain in Flanders. Is it relevant to look at Berlin in the same way?

In Flanders, 90 percent of the heritage for the coming century is already present. This means we will have to be precise about how to develop the remaining 10 percent, and that we will have to ask ourselves whether the consumption of any more free space is really necessary. Instead of developing architecture further as a discipline that consumes space, we should optimize that space which already exists. It isn't necessary to use up yet more space, unless we can enhance it by organizing it in a certain way.

Berlin is a very large city that still has a lot of open space. The city is known for its residual space, for its relative surplus of public space, and for a culture in which public space also plays an important role for its residents. They relate to these spaces in a remarkably spontaneous way. But the city is becoming increasingly built up and finds itself at a turning point. Care must be taken that the share of indeterminate and vague space does not come under too much pressure from the built and the accompanying traditional public space.

Can places that are as yet still indeterminate be given the function of "undetermined space"? Or should they be transformed in an interesting way into qualitative public space in the more traditional sense of the word?

Can Tempelhofer Feld play a role here?

One of the starting points of your research was the relationship between the planned and the unplanned and the balance found in the temporary "in between" situation. Are you planning to promote one or the other as more or less desirable in a future vision for such a place? The danger of the current polemic around Tempelhofer Feld is that it zooms in on the distinction between the planned and unplanned in favor of a certain conviction.

Are you referring to the way in which the 100% Tempelhofer Feld action group is diametrically opposed to the plans of the Berlin Senate?

I find the relationship between the planned and the unplanned problematic when it is misused to weigh future visions against each other. This can often lead to a situation in which the urban planner who is advising the authorities gets pushed into the "planned" corner. A design can in itself allow for the unplanned. The quality of a good design lies in *not excluding* certain future developments, as well as deciding what will be the guiding factors for things that *have to* happen. An integral part of the designer's job is to think about how actions play a guiding role. That means we have to try and imagine what will happen. In our current age, when there's frequently a strong marketing and communication message behind the design, there's no place left for that imagination process. We cannot relate the design thinking solely to the limited interpretation of the planned versus the unplanned.

In the long term, leaving an area indeterminate rarely leads to a high-quality urban space. It requires precision to design a space that allows for the unplanned. Artist and architect Luc Deleu, for example, places great emphasis on structuring contexts: he organizes urban space using a number of powerfully developed spatial decisions in which there is room left for the unexpected, an urban space to be used as every individual sees fit. The design is very important precisely because it provides a context for the interplay between the planned and the unplanned.

What do you think about the plans proposed by the Berlin Senate for Tempelhofer Feld?

The Tempelhofer Feld situation is very specific: an exceptionally large and relatively central space suddenly loses its function and thus acquires a sort of temporary state.

The future plans that the Senate proposes may seem unique, but they are actually very traditional. They are part of a design culture that is aimed at an image that is only unequivocally of high quality when it has a spectacular aspect as its final target: an ultimate urban park where everyone will be happy. This is very obvious from the notes in the preliminary draft. Tempelhofer Freiheit is being promoted as something that other cities will envy.[2] That kind of marketing jargon has become inherent to virtually all urban developments and architecture projects in the last decade. They always capitalize on a number of market logics, which in visual and architectural terms are at odds with the qualities of the space.

The temporary use and the projected future plans are very distinct from one another. The insight you gain from walking around Tempelhofer Feld now renders that tangible. The plan presents a final purpose for a terrain that is still evolving, a space whose role in the future and whose significance for the city is still unfolding. Because this space has suddenly opened up in the city, there is an opportunity to realize a new ambition for that area and to prove that it can now serve as something new for the city. This can only be done by consulting the various parties who might benefit from it, not necessarily only in financial terms.

In that sense I think the proposal offered by the landscape architects GROSS. MAX. is inadequate. It is not that it is spatially weak, however—the problem is rooted in the way the authorities formulated the task.

What kind of benefit could this sort of terrain generate?

I'm thinking of qualities that at first glance go unnoticed, such as collective benefits rather than private gain. Tempelhofer Feld is a perfect place for the less traditional needs of a city. The area has a lot of potential in terms of ecological structure and biodiversity. You immediately sense how unique this open space is in contrast with the density of a contemporary city, and how important emptiness can be in this context. Temporary use of indeterminate spaces allows people the opportunity to innovate, for example by developing local economies that are closer to the lives of the working-class neighborhoods in the area. These can be seized by less-defined classes within the urban

2 "Tempelhofer Freiheit is a blessing for Berlin, and one that will make other cities simply go green with envy." Michael Müller, then senator for Urban Development and the Environment, cited in a Tempelhofer Freiheit leaflet "Park Landscape Development," collected at Tempelhofer Feld, July 19, 2012.

population as a step in their personal development. It is a function of the city that has always been very important. It lies at the heart of the global movement of migration from the countryside to the city, where it is the wish of these migrants to get a start in life with a new trade, a new skill, or a new future. Such things are more difficult to plan in advance and are more fragile in terms of calculating the income from such a space.

You said just then that the problem has partly to do with the way the authorities formulated the assignment for the designers. Can you elaborate on that?

In recent decades, the designer has often been engaged at too late a stage and for too short a time in the process of developing our living environment. As such, his role has been degraded to that of a decorator of the city. Design-based thinking and the role of the architect and the urban planner should all be a part of the process much earlier. The designer could then take on an intermediary role and apply design-based thinking and the power of imagination to bring the stakeholders together. Not just around one image of what a certain area should be but around the various layers, qualities, services, and possible futures. As such, the architect becomes a mediator who guides the process using certain objective facts about the physical space in question, thus ensuring that the knowledge about that specific space is shared. The designer can then help steer certain choices the commissioning party is responsible for making.

You tried to fill that void with Architecture Workroom Brussels?

The role of the designer as process supervisor, as moderator, as mediator, as intermediary is indeed something that we have developed as a profession, from the conviction that there are a number of societal challenges high on the political agenda that could be better addressed if design-based thinking was employed. On the basis of various kinds of campaigns—ranging from more intrinsic, research-related, curatorial campaigns to brainstorming—we tried to introduce new themes into the heart of the public debate in various contexts. In this way, the vision of those who are entitled to make decisions in a certain process is expanded, and the right topics are put on the agenda. On the one hand, we do this by taking on the role of supervisor, helping the commissioning party to develop the necessary planning, phasing, timing, and methodology in a process. On the other hand, we are active participants in the cultural world, whereby we try to stir up public opinion through publications, exhibitions, lectures, and debates.

With Architecture Workroom Brussels you want to create contexts in which the better architectural practices get the space to innovate. How can this be achieved?

In the first phase, we try to collect existing knowledge on a certain issue, or at least a selection of the existing knowledge, and objectify it in a certain way. This is then put on the table as basic content or as shared knowledge. Then we bring together the stakeholders, the so-called "owners of the problem," ranging from certain authorities, institutions, and interest groups to owners of particular sites, to consider this information. Every actor who might benefit from a certain spatial-development process is invited. This is done in parallel with the meeting of designers to consider that same information. By using practices that are characteristic of the design discipline—cartography, sketching, drawing—the spatial translation of the problem is linked to the data that has been collected on the specific situation.

Sharing the elementary basic knowledge about a certain problem with all the stakeholders is actually a very important part of this process. Strangely enough, it appears from the experiments conducted that this is already revolutionary compared to the way such processes used to be carried out. Sometimes it seems so obvious who the parties involved in a certain issue and certain space are, but these people rarely come together around one table. This could be the start of a very different relationship in the arena of decision-making on certain futures for a city or region.

Can this methodology be projected onto Tempelhofer Feld?

It can indeed be projected onto evolutions involving Tempelhofer Feld. I get the impression that a number of projects in this direction have already been developed in the past but at some point have not gone ahead. I refer to the role that agencies like raumlabor and Urban Catalyst studio have played in helping the Berlin Senate to develop a future vision. Because they were no longer regularly involved in the meetings, there was a limit to the insight among all the actors who might make a contribution to the future of Tempelhofer Feld. As a result, the process evolved into a virtual zoning plan by the developer and commissiong party. The development of a platform for an evolutionary social feeling, a project that related to everyone, quietly disappeared from play.

I think it's essential, where possible, to have a variety of people around the table again, perhaps not for the whole Tempelhofer Feld project but certainly for parts of it. Through research by design, they can be engaged to project already formulated aspects of the issue onto that physical space.

In reality the opposite is often generated, namely a polemic around a certain future. It is relatively easy to mobilize a lot of people very quickly in favor of or against a certain issue. The problem is that this is then expressed and understood as a sort of vacillation for or against one or the other project, partly because of the mediatization of society. I'm not calling for participation and social debate to be neutralized, but our work with Architecture Workroom is about defusing the problem of polemicization, namely the creation of a war of conflicting opinions. Instead, we start from the same problem and together look for a solution that can evolve into a layered and nuanced vision of the future.

This is precisely what Benjamin's photography and the reflection on the current use of Tempelhofer Feld in your research underpins. I think it's crucial that the now relatively simplified composition of owners of the problem is exposed, and that more actors are involved in the future of this area. Then we can refer back to discussions about the ecological and social value of Tempelhofer Feld. In addition, in such a case the historical value is often reduced to "museumization," reduced down to a tourist attraction, while, especially in Berlin, history and memories have a much broader function in an urban context. Other aspects such as the socioeconomic importance of urban development, the problem of gentrification, training courses, employment through local economies, etc., must all be included in this renewed agenda.

What did this approach lead to in the case of *The Ambition of the Territory*?

It seemed that the various players who were instrumental in deciding what to do with the residual space in Flanders, ranging from the Vlaamse Landmaatschappij (Flemish Land Agency), Agentschap voor Natuur en Bos (Flemish Agency for Nature and Forests), Bond Beter Leefmilieu (Federation for a Better Environment), and the Boerenbond (The Belgian Farmers Union) to the various nature associations, were often all lined up for a struggle over that open space. In reality, they have common interests in strengthening this open space so that it as a kind of natural system that serves the urban system. During *The Ambition of the Territory* exhibition, we were pleasantly surprised by the constructive debate that arose, for example, between the nature conservation movement and the farming lobby. On the basis of the preliminary studies, we were able to show that there is a lot to be gained by starting with what can be done together with that space, instead of seeing who has a claim on it. In those conversations we completely overturned the question of who is most entitled to consume that space. Instead, we exposed what that space has to offer in the form of shared benefits.

The cultural setting where that conversation took place was very important. How did this influence the project?

We were expected to put on an exhibition in deSingel, the arts campus in Antwerp. Instead of a copy of the installation in Venice, we created a workshop setting in the exhibition space. We then invited the various players concerned with the Flemish territory and facilitated a conversation.

In a cultural and artistic environment, you almost automatically create a sort of space for free thinking. When people come in, they no longer feel backed up by their institutional background or their traditional positions and they automatically start thinking about the problems in a personal or humane way. This led to new relationships between all the actors involved in each particular problem. The cultural space was interpreted here as a social space, a free zone where there was room for experimentation and a renewal for a range of ideas.

Are there any qualifiers or problems related to such an approach?

The sticking point is the translation of the insight built up in this "free zone" into actual processes outside the contours of the zone. The challenge is to give our societal organization—the various administrative bodies, authorities, and sectors—the necessary tools to put this spatial vision into practice. This has to happen on a communal and regional level, as well as a national and European level.

In addition to that, of course, the many designers who have to come up with answers to the various urban and spatial-design assignments must have enough expertise to automatically integrate the nuances and the different constituent aspects of those innovative reflections into their designs. The training of young architects, the debate within the discipline, and the promotion of certain new methods, thinking, and discourse within the practice of design must receive sufficient backing. Here too the interest groups, civil society, the cultural world, architecture, and urban planning all have a crucial role to play. When the political vision leads to the right project definition for the question at hand, there must be a sufficient exchange of knowledge in design practice so that the candidate designers are able to understand the framework of that vision. Consequently, rather than "as many as possible" spatial designers, it ought to be "as varied a group as possible" who should be involved in such a process from the very beginning. This could also be relevant for Tempelhofer Feld. The moment a design process is arranged, the designers that are called in must be able to integrate the subtlety and sensitivity of the temporariness of Tempelhofer Feld into the constituent problems that are presented.

The project that raumlabor and Urban Catalyst studio developed for Tempelhofer Feld was built around that sort of open design process. So why wasn't that idea used in the end?

It just goes to show that we should always be aware that such processes are at a certain point about political choices, and about a vision of society held by the people in power.

Those who have to make the final decision on the methodology of development were ultimately not convinced. That's probably because there was too little knowledge and expertise concerning such open design processes among the major policy-makers and actors involved. It is seen as a complex process and they don't believe that this extra complexity would be of added value at the end of the road and in the long term.

At Architecture Workroom, we are fully committed to dealing with and reducing this lack of knowledge. The analysis of successful as well as less successful processes from similar developments in other cities is an important part of that. The useful elements of this analysis are documented and translated in terms of the people involved in the process at hand, in particular the policy-makers and the public's opinion.

Should the architect extend his field of action into politics?

We consider the link between architecture and politics to be essential. The goal of creating a sustainable and qualitative space fit for the future is connected to the model of our current iteration of society. Architecture is supported by politics and its raison d'être is the organization of society. Spatial organization is heavily influenced by political ideologies and decisions. If we want to intervene efficiently in this area, then close ties with politics are vital. Design thinking must contribute to the way we shape our living environment, transcending a specific ideological context linked to a specific political party.

Design practice should be engaged in all parts of society. It is precisely in the connection with other social processes that architecture can make such an interesting contribution to the organization of our cities and our society.

Biographies

Markus Bader (DE) is an architect and co-founder of raumlabor. He studied architecture at the Berlin Technical University and art at the University of Arts in Berlin and is a graduate of the Bartlett School of Architecture in London.

Bader is a visiting professor of Urban Practice at the University of Kassel, in the department of Architecture, City Planning, and Landscape Architecture. His areas of expertise include the interconnection of art, architecture, and urbanism.

raumlabor are a group of architects based in Berlin, Germany, who came together in 1999 in response to the rapid and unrestrained development of the city following the fall of the Berlin Wall. Their playful approach critiques this dominant mode of architectural production. Their projects try to open up a space of communication and negotiation in which relations can be made and conflicts played out. For them, architecture is first and foremost a social phenomenon. Raumlabor has developed projects for, among others, ZKM – Center for Art and Media, Kampnagel Hamburg, and the Architecture Biennale in Venice.

Eric Corijn (BE) is professor emeritus of social and cultural geography at the Free University of Brussels (VUB). He is the founder of COSMOPOLIS, Centre for Urban Research, vice-chair of the Brussels Studies Institute, and director of the Brussels Academy. He is the author of more than 250 publications. His latest book is *The Brussels Reader: A Small World City to Become the Capital of Europe* (VUB Press, 2013).

Kenny Cupers (BE) obtained his PhD at Harvard University and is associate professor of history and theory of architecture and urbanism at the University of Basel. He is the author of *The Social Project: Housing Postwar France* (University of Minnesota Press, 2014) and editor of *Use Matters: An Alternative History of Architecture* (Routledge, 2013). His published work concerns the relationship between modern architecture and the welfare state, participatory urbanism and the aesthetics of the everyday, sociological knowledge production and geographical concepts in architecture and urban planning, and relationships between landscape, governance, and modern selfhood. His most recent book project, provisionally entitled "Modernism and the Environment: An Epistemological History," examines how environmental thinking has shaped twentieth-century architecture and urban planning.

Lieven De Cauter (BE) is a philosopher, art historian, writer, and activist. He teaches philosophy of culture at the Department and Faculty of Architecture at the University of Leuven and RITCS School of Arts, in Brussels. He has written and edited several books on contemporary art, experience and modernity, Walter Benjamin, and more recently on architecture, the city, and politics. He also publishes poems, philosophical columns, statements, pamphlets, and opinion pieces in newspapers and online. His most recently translated publications are *The Capsular Civilization: On the City in the Age of Fear* (NAI Publishers, 2004); *Heterotopia and the City: Public Space in a Postcivil Society* (Routledge, 2008, coedited with Michiel Dehaene); *Art and Activism in the Age of Globalization*, (NAI Publishers, 2011, coedited with Karel Vanhaesebrouck and Ruben De Roo); and *Entropic Empire: On the City of Man in the Age of Disaster* (nai010 publishers, 2012).

Roeland Dudal (BE) is co-founder of Architecture Workroom Brussels. He teaches architectural design at the Faculty of Architecture of the University of Leuven at Campus Ghent and Brussels. From 2004 to 2009, he was project leader for the Flemish Architecture Institute in Antwerp. He produced the exhibition series *35m3 young architecture* and realized the exhibition *Mare Meum* (International Architecture Biennale Rotterdam 2005, Ghent 2005, Ostend 2006). In 2008, he was production coordinator of the Belgian Pavilion at the 11th International Architecture Biennale in Venice.

Architecture Workroom Brussels is a think-and-do tank for innovation in architecture, urban planning, and other fields related to spatial development. They promote the role and the meaning of spatial design in the formulation of a response to the social problems inherent in a rapidly urbanizing world. Architecture Workroom Brussels functions as a pivotal platform between designers, politicians, administrators, and citizens. In 2008, Architecture Workroom curated the exhibition *Building for Brussels* and coordinated the project City Trajectory Brussels Canal. In 2012, Architecture Workroom was a member of the curatorial team for the exhibition *Making City – 5th International Architecture Biennale Rotterdam*. From 2014 on, Architecture Workroom has been a part of the research-by-design team for the projects Eurodelta 2030–2100 and Metropolitan Coast Landscape 2100.

Andrej Holm (DE) is a social scientist working at the Institute for Urban and Regional Sociology at the Humboldt University in Berlin. His research interests include gentrification, comparative housing policy, and European urban policy. With a focus on socio-structural transformation and administrative political control mechanisms of urban renewal, he has analyzed most poignantly the connections between (sub-)cultural and symbolic evaluations to real-estate commodification. Aside from his professional research interests, Holm is active in various neighborhood and tenant initiatives. His work includes research projects and publications such as *Die Restrukturierung des Raumes. Stadterneuerung der 90er Jahre in Ostberlin: Interessen und Machtverhältnisse* (Transcript, 2006); *Wir bleiben alle! Gentrifizierung – Städtische Konflikte um Aufwertung und Verdrängung* (Unrast Verlag, 2010); and *Reclaim Berlin: Soziale Kämpfe in der neoliberalen Stadt* (Assoziaton A, 2014).

Markus Miessen (DE) is an architect, spatial consultant, and writer. He received his PhD from the Centre for Research Architecture at Goldsmiths in 2015. As initiator of the *Participation* tetralogy, his work revolves around questions of critical spatial practice, institution building, and spatial politics. His practice, Studio Miessen, is currently working on projects for and with Artsonje Seoul, Witte de With Rotterdam, Kunstverein in Hamburg, CCA Tel Aviv, Kosovo National Gallery, EACC Castelló, IMA Brisbane, the artist Hito Steyerl, the design collective New Tendency, and a residential project in Los Angeles. The studio's largest project to date is a strategic framework design for a former NATO military site in Germany. In 2008, Miessen founded the Winter School Middle East Kuwait. He has previously taught at the Berlage Institute Rotterdam and the Architectural Association London and has been a fellow at Harvard University. Most recently, Miessen has held an endowed professorship for critical spatial practice at the Städelschule Frankfurt, has directed a studio at HEAD Geneva, and is currently professor of practice at the University of Southern California, Los Angeles.

Philipp Oswalt (DE) is an architect and writer. He has worked for the architectural journal *Arch+* and the Office for Metropolitan Architecture/Rem Koolhaas in Rotterdam and was visiting professor for design at the Technical University Cottbus. From 2001 to 2003, he initiated and coordinated Urban Catalysts, the European research project on temporality in urban space, which was later developed into a platform of the same name. He was chief curator of the international research and exhibition project Shrinking Cities for the German cultural foundation and co-curator of *Volkspalast 2004*. From 2009 until 2014, he was director of the Bauhaus Dessau Foundation. Besides his ongoing work as an independent architect, he is currently professor for architecture theory and design at the University of Kassel. He is the author of *Shrinking Cities* (Hatje Cantz Publishers, 2006, coedited with Wolfgang Kil) and *Urban Catalyst: The Power of Temporary Use* (Dom Publishers, 2013, coedited with Klaus Overmeyer and Philipp Misselwitz).

Urban Catalyst was founded in 2003 by Philipp Misselwitz, Philipp Oswalt, and Klaus Overmeyer. It developed from the European research project of the same name that explored strategies for temporary use in residual urban areas. As an interdisciplinary platform for research, projects, public interventions, conferences, exhibitions, and publications, Urban Catalyst aims to foster public discourse on contemporary urban issues and develop concepts and strategies for planners and architects. In 2003, co-founder Klaus Overmeyer also launched Studio Urban Catalyst, which in 2012 became the Urban Catalyst studio office partnership.

About the authors:

Benjamin Deboosere (BE) received his master's degree in film directing from the RITCS School of Arts in Brussels. Deboosere now primarily works with artists and cultural and social institutions as a filmmaker, editor, screenwriter, and photographer.

Wouter De Raeve (BE) studied landscape architecture at the Erasmus University College in Brussels. He is active as a spatial practitioner, artist, and curator.

Acknowledgments

Benjamin Deboosere and Wouter De Raeve would like to thank the following individuals and institutions:

Anne König, **Jan Wenzel**, **Ames Gerould**, and **Robert Stürzl** from Spector Books.

The Commission for Architecture and Design within the Government of Flanders' Agency for Arts and Heritage for their financial support in helping to realize this publication.

Susanne Kriemann, **Aleksander Komarov**, and **Ilka Tödt** from **AIR Berlin Alexanderplatz.**

Team International Arts within the Government of Flanders' Agency for Arts and Heritage for giving us the opportunity to take part in their International Residencies in the Arts program.

Andrej Holm, **Eric Corijn**, **Kenny Cupers**, **Lieven De Cauter**, **Markus Bader**, **Markus Miessen**, **Philipp Oswalt**, and **Roeland Dudal** for their time, effort, and insights.

A warm thank you to all the people of Tempelhofer Feld that were kind enough to allow themselves to be photographed.

Elisabeth Mohr and **Lynn Tytgat** for copyediting, translating, peer reviewing, advising, and supporting us throughout the whole process of making this publication.

Tobias Wenig for his enduring sense of commitment and creativity in designing this publication.

Roeland Dudal and **Susanne Kriemann** for their support, advice, and guidance during the course of this project.

Manuel Aalbers, **Jens Aerts**, **Brecht Baert**, **Gregory Ball**, **Herman Barges**, **Wouter Bervoets**, **Charles Blondeel**, **Hans Bruch Jr.**, **Livia Cahn**, **Elise Candry**, **Luna Catteeuw**, **Sanne Claeys**, **Simon Cowper**, **Sarah Deboosere**, **Patrick Deboosere**, **Benjamin De Cleen**, **Ken De Cooman**, **Stefan De Corte**, **Kris Dejonckheere**, **Luk De Raeve**, **Jorg De Vriese**, **Anna Faroqhi**, **Mascha Fehse**, **Pieterjan Grandry**, **Britta Grell**, **Stephanie Han**, **Katrien Hebbelinck**, **Frauke Hell**, **Melanie Henneger**, **Paoletta Holst**, **Hannes Jung**, **Valentina Karga**, **Kolja Kinnebrock**, **Katrien Laenen**, **Patrick Lennon**, **Jef Leyssens**, **Thomas Lovegrove**, **Thomas J. Martin**, **Matthias** from Café Engels, **Laura Muyldermans**, **Node Center for Curatorial Studies**, **Justine Liv Olausson**, **Helly Parsons**, **Rob Ritzen**, **Raphael Rogenmoser**, **Lisa Schouppe**, **Tim Sontheimer**, **Stavros Stavrides**, **Kalie Stieda**, **Lilli Unger**, **Steyn Van Assche**, **Jaklien Vandermeulen**, **Yannick Van Keer**, **Lieselot Vanhoof**, **Tom Van Imschoot**, **Veerle Wenes**, and **Ria Willem**

Edited by Benjamin Deboosere, Wouter De Raeve
Graphic design: Tobias Wenig
Translation: Gregory Ball, Patrick Lennon
Copyediting: Gregory Ball, Ames Gerould, Patrick Lennon
Proofreading: Simon Cowper
Printing and binding: Pöge Druck, Leipzig

Published by
Spector Books
Harkortstraße 10
04107 Leipzig
www.spectorbooks.com

Distribution
Germany, Austria: GVA, Gemeinsame Verlagsauslieferung Göttingen GmbH&Co. KG, www.gva-verlage.de
Switzerland: AVA Verlagsauslieferung AG, www.ava.ch
France, Belgium: Interart Paris, www.interart.fr
UK: Central Books Ltd, www.centralbooks.com
USA, Canada: RAM Publications+Distribution Inc., www.rampub.com
Australia, New Zealand: Perimeter Distribution, www.perimeterdistribution.com
Other countries: Motto Distribution, www.mottodistribution.com

First edition

Printed in Germany

ISBN 978-3-944669-64-9

Supported by the Commission for Architecture and Design within the Government of Flanders' Agency for Arts and Heritage

Flanders
State of the Art